Real Women
Real Wisdom

Real Women
Real Wisdom

a journey into the feminine soul

edited by

Maureen Hovenkotter

Gray Wings Press, LLC
Milwaukie, Oregon
2011

Library of Congress Control Number: 2011936293

ISBN 978-0-615-47680-3

Dedication

*On behalf of all the women contributors,
this book is dedicated to our loved ones:
those still with us and those who
have gone ahead on the journey.*

Contents

Barbara Underwood Scharff, Motherhood and Daughterhood: Love and Goodbye   7

Karen Nettler, Suffering and Our Image of God   22

Marie Goretti Abijuru, Home in God's Hands   28

Cheryl Rohret, To Turn and to Fly with Love   40

Katie Hennessy, Mission Country   49

Suzanne Dillard Burke, Journey through Grief   57

Karen Gatens, Blessed with Blindness   70

Sherold Barr, What Death Can Teach Us About Life   81

Lola Scobey, Even Good Girls Get the Blues   89

Marilyn Kirvin, Put the Key in the Ignition   113

Gale Cunningham, Goodbye, Again   125

Marilyn Jaeger Veomett, "This Is Not What I Expected!"   137

Beth Patterson, Closer Than Our Own Skin   150

Gayle Yamasaki, One Day at a Time   156

Charlotte Bloebaum, Dancing Through The Storm   168

Anonymous, God Writes Straight with Crooked Lines   184

Maureen Hovenkotter, Finding the Grace In Loneliness   195

Contributors Notes   208

Saying Yes

When was it?
The time, the place remain an
Unmarked grave for my old life.
But I wonder . . .
Was it while watching waves
Breathing in, breathing out,
Kissing the shore, then sliding back
To the horizon, taking bits of my heart?
Or gazing at golden fingers of sunlight
Stretching down through fog-wrapped firs,
Beckoning, welcoming?
Perhaps a summer night filled with awe and
Shooting stars. They came after a dazzling sky
Of orchid and magenta
Darkened to violet, then indigo.
Or maybe that Christmas Eve.
Walking home from Midnight Mass we found
Rhododendrons blooming.
Did I surrender while holding my newborn
Grandson resting on my heart?
Rather, I think it was some quiet moment
Unnoticed, unremarkable
Except for my quiet yielding yes after
So many maybes and not yets.
But, Faithful Lover, you never gave up and,
In Love, you kept inviting.
Finally, one day, it was time; I was ready
For such a fierce love.
"Come, follow me," you whispered.
"Leave all behind and follow me."
And this time, I said yes
And knew I would never be the same.
                    © Maureen Hovenkotter

Introduction

*Where morning dawns and evening fades you
call forth songs of joy. – Psalm 65:8*

IN MY 61 YEARS on this planet I have come to accept that almost everything can change. In a heartbeat, disaster can strike, leaving lives turned upside-down and inside out. Your spouse, a child or other loved one can die suddenly or become involved in life-threatening behavior. You can walk out of a doctor's office stunned by a devastating medical prognosis that will jeopardize your physical, mental and financial health, if not your very life. The place you've worked for 20 years can become the victim of a bad economy or bring on a new manager who decides you don't fit in any more, and suddenly you are looking for work and questioning everything in your life. One day your spouse can announce that he or she has found someone else and your long-time marriage, that you believed would last forever, is over.

Life changes can also be self-induced and can be just as sudden, or can follow months or years of introspection. You might realize in conversation with a trusted friend, after reading something thought-provoking, or even through your dreams that the path you have been following is no longer right for you, if it ever was.

There is no insurance that will protect us from change. It is inevitable; whether it comes to us or we seek it out. We can allow it to make us angry and bitter people, or we can find grace and gift in change. Although almost always painful, change can bring about transformation and growth, greater awareness and compassion, if we open our hearts to those possibilities.

In *Real Women, Real Wisdom* 17 women share their reflections on life, loss, love and mystery. Most have faced very difficult and dark times of change and fought their way through, back into light—often a brighter, truer light than before. They openly and generously share their stories of moving forward, sometimes with nothing more than blind faith to guide them.

One of the contributors pointed out that the chapters share much suffering. But the stories bring the reader to a deeper understanding of "how we hold together a good God and the reality of suffering . . . each woman came up with a rather different approach to that question, but in some ways, the answers are also similar." Though different, I think the stories are woven with a common thread of acceptance and trust.

Many of the contributors are women I have come to know and love through my Roman Catholic faith community in Portland; I have valued their wisdom and believe it holds great value for others. Others were recommended to me by friends, by my spiritual director and by the women themselves.

At times it almost seemed that the book was taking on a life of its own, going where it wanted and needed to and not necessarily where I thought it should go. Some of the writers experienced a similar phenomenon: starting out in one direction but finding their stories needed to travel in another direction completely. I believe all of them found growth, revelation and peace in sharing their stories and their thoughts: writing their reflections to share with others became part of the journey.

Several of the women shared with me that working on their chapter was a difficult, very emotional, but also healing experience. It allowed them to revisit a dark time and look at it from a different perspective, with greater understanding. In the process of writing, they realized how much they have grown as a result of these challenges. One woman wrote: "I ate a whole bag of Kettle chips and half of a giant tub of red licorice revisiting the darkness of this time in my life. I've realized that now that I'm in the light—whew!—I don't want to go back. It's been a long, hard journey to get here." Rebirth always is.

While most of the writers come from a Catholic or other traditional Christian background, some have also explored a different spiritual path. All are women who believe in and trust a very loving, forgiving Divine Creator. This in spite of some very difficult challenges in their lives and subsequent doubts about how a loving God could allow such suffering, human cruelty or natural disasters to happen—doubts that most people struggle with at some point in their lives. Most of the women have found that their journey to a deeper connection to the Divine moving in their lives and the world opens them up to a wider recognition of the mystery: that is, they come to a realization and acceptance of the Unknowable and learn to trust in that mystery many of us call God.

A few of the women who have contributed chapters are already published authors; some have web pages or blogs where they share their thoughts, opinions and reflections. But several are not trained as writers or communicators, and it was a great stretch for them to organize and share their stories. Some have training in divinity, spirituality, theology, counseling, spiritual direction and have worked closely with great suffering. Others have only their own life experiences to share.

It took great courage for all of them to share publicly what are deeply private experiences and thoughts, to open themselves to criticism and be vulnerable. One woman wanted to share her journey in learning to cope with a traumatic experience from many years ago but wasn't comfortable sharing her name. In other cases, the names of individuals in the stories have been changed to protect their identity and privacy.

Each chapter stands alone and reflects the personal experiences and views of its author, views not necessarily shared by the publisher or other authors. I believe all the women handle difficult subjects with great compassion, fairness, openness and love. Ultimately I think we are all called to accept people and their personal faith and life journeys as their own and to leave the judging to God who, I believe, is a much more gentle and loving judge than any of us can ever hope to be. As God reminded Samuel in the Old Testament: "Not as humans see does God see." 1 Samuel 16:7. For the One we call God, that life energy that imbues all of creation with beauty and joy, is indeed God and Creator to all of us, no matter what our faith journey, our creed, our belief system.

Most of the contributors to this book are women who have few, if any, opportunities to share their life experience, wisdom and stories beyond a very small circle. My hope in putting together this book was to allow their beautiful stories to shine some of the light they have found into the lives of others who might need a glimmer of hope to get through their own dark journeys. As one woman suggested: these are stories that needed to be told. I am privileged to have been the instrument that allowed these wise voices to be heard.

Acknowledgements:

First and foremost I express my deepest gratitude to the 17 women who share their personal stories within the pages of this book. Thank you for trusting me with your stories. This book was created out of love and to be of service to others, not for commercial success. In my opinion, the women who have contributed have already made it a success because of their own healing experiences during their writing. I have been inspired and found it a graced experience getting to know them each more deeply through their writing. They give me hope.

My additional thanks go to my good friend Marilyn Kirvin who, despite her own life-threatening, devastating illness, found the time to help with reading and editing. Her astute observations, thoughtful questions, and ongoing support throughout the project have been incredibly helpful.

Another contributor, Marilyn Veomett, also spent hours combing through the document for spelling, typing or other mistakes and offered critical suggestions and feedback. I'm also thankful to Marilyn Kirvin and our friend, Janet Buck, for helping me refine and hone the message of my chapter for the book. Likewise I extend thanks to the friends and loved ones of all the women who have helped them refine their stories, given advice and support.

I am grateful to the poets who gave us permission to share their beautiful words. Thank you, Danna Fauld and Kaylin Haught.

I thank my spiritual director, Jack Kennedy, who believed in the project enough to connect me with several of the women who have contributed stories.

Marissa "Tora" Stark of ToraIllustration created a beautiful cover, using a photo I took that includes some of the women authors. Karen Gatens, another contributor, provided valuable suggestions and advice regarding the cover art and graphics.

And thank YOU for reading the book. I hope it will bring additional light, understanding and joy into your life.

Maureen Hovenkotter

Motherhood and Daughterhood: Love and Goodbye

by Barbara Underwood Scharff

WE ALL BELONG to someone, or the Great Someone, but we often forget. As women—daughters all, mothers some—I want to remember the special and complex quality of belonging conferred by the roles of female kinship. We are a mother each time we parent a child. We are a daughter twice, in our childhood as we receive our mother's care, and in our adulthood as we give our aging mothers care. I have had the supreme privilege of experiencing the kinship inherent in both motherhood and daughterhood.

Reflections on Motherhood

Before my husband Gary and I got married in 1979, we omitted an important conversation. We never talked about having children. Two years into our marriage, I produced a series of radio shows while working at NBC in San Francisco exploring the subject of "the biological clock." My guests were women ages 20 to 40 who'd made divergent decisions about birthing—or no decision (and time became their decider). Together we asked: Do I want children? Can I have children? Am I glad I had children, or chose not to? How would I feel looking back over my life if I chose not to have children? What are the risks and hoped-for rewards of choosing parenthood? At the end of these four shows, I knew in my gut what I wanted. I couldn't imagine looking back over my life not having had children.

I've received some wonderful Mother's Day cards over the years from my three children. A shoe-box full of these special sentiments lies in my closet. But motherhood is not a sentimental journey. It is not lived in pastels, but in primary colors. Whether my perspective is as a mother or as the child of a mother, I look on motherhood as a daring journey, a patient and uncertain one filled with unknown hellos and good-byes, filled with times of desolation and immeasurable purpose and consolation. It is nothing less than a faithful, bountiful, tiring, muddling, hoping, panoramic trek.

On Mother's Day 1982, my husband Gary and I learned that we were pregnant for the first time. With this discovery came a torrent of feelings. Incredulity. Anticipation. I was downright scared, frightened for any innocent being entering a world so threatened by crisis and loss. I was worried for the health of the baby. It all seemed out of my control. And the responsibility of parenthood—how were Gary and I going to learn the delicate art of parenting in nine short months? I couldn't imagine my body changing so drastically to grow and shelter another human being, someone who had never existed before. Would my tremulous heart catch up to the enormous reality?

There is an old Irish saying: "It is in the shelter of each other that people live." It is literally in the shelter of the Mother that we all start out life. We share the same bodily origin, a species kinship, as we develop from seed and egg in a dark vessel and make our way through the maternal portal into the light.

As I reflect upon my pregnancies with each of my three beautiful children—Elana, Jesse and Thomas—I think of hope, faith and surrender. Hope, because new life is stunning and affirming. Birth and parenting is an act of faith in a world with such profound uncertainties. And the surrender is to natural and spiritual forces that trump the human mind and will.

I remember staring at each newborn, amazed by her singular presence, wondering how he was put together so intricately, where she'd come from, and how it came to be that I was on earth to steward—for awhile—his or her sacred being.

That surrender, that sacrifice is not an easy or predictable road. It is filled with trial and error, frustration, occasional frights and loss, a hefty dose of dumb luck, and daily awakenings and surprises. My husband and I were reminded of our rookie status by the nurse in the hospital in Berkeley, California where I'd given birth to my first-born, Elana. As we were leaving the hospital, the nurse whispered to our two-day old infant: "Elana, be good to your parents. They don't have a clue what they're doing."

But thank you, God, for throwing in some humor along the rocky parenting road. Thank goodness children are given the ingredient of unselfconscious charm—because that's what so often saves their skins. And when they learn to use words—brace yourself—those utterly original comments made me think they were little reincarnated beings from other galaxies.

A few vignettes give a taste of the salt and pepper of raising young ones. I'll never forget the time when Jesse, our second child, was two years old and got the hiccoughs and they wouldn't go away.

Gary said to Jesse, "Sometimes you can get rid of hiccoughs if you hold your breath." So Jesse, in his literal way, blew his breath into his hands and held it!

When I was eight months pregnant with Thomas, my youngest, I was washing Elana's feet before bed one night. She was six, and out of the blue she asked, "Why is that baby in you?"

I answered obliquely, not quite prepared to be honest, and said, "Well, he'll be coming out soon and then you'll have another brother to love."

"No," Elana insisted impatiently, daring me. "I don't want to know that he's coming out. I want to know how he got in there!"

One evening Jesse and I were on the sofa reading a book; he narrowly missed kicking my pregnant belly, so I took his shoes off. Later in the week, I told Jesse that I just felt the baby kick me from inside.

Jesse exclaimed, "That's ok, Mom, he doesn't have any shoes on."

Once Thomas was sucking a jaw breaker candy his brother had given him called a dinosaur egg. Thomas had been keeping it in his mouth for a long time. I started to worry he might choke on it, and I asked him about it.

He shot back with expectancy in his eyes, "I can't chew it. I'm waiting for it to hatch!"

In 1993, my middle son, Jesse, and I were walking side by side to Grant Park near our home in Northeast Portland. I was a full-time parent for a few years, and he was in second grade, with a marked flash of honesty.

"Mom," he said, gripping my hand, "you were a really good student in college weren't you?"

I answered yes, and then expected maybe a little compliment.

Instead Jesse said, "Why didn't you grow up and do something important with your life? You know being a mom won't make you rich or famous!"

Wow! This hit me hard. It shouldn't have, but it made me feel unworthy. And I thought about it for weeks. In fact, Jesse had named a dissatisfaction, an angst I had been carrying for several months. I wasn't, after all, earning a paycheck or building a career, and I often found myself questioning my value. Gary was working 12 hour days away from home as a busy professional, and other people all around me seemed to be doing so many more important things with their lives than changing diapers, cleaning up chaos, calming melt-downs and refereeing sibling squabbles.

Little kids are wired for self-centeredness, as they should be. They aren't there to buck you up as a struggling parent trying to answer your own self-identity or personal destiny questions.

In my insecurities, I struggled between what our culture tells us about ourselves—that we are deficient and lacking in one way or another—and what my faith teaches is the truth about ourselves—that we are exactly what God had in mind when he created us. But as a mom, faced with my side-line status, my imperfections, my impatience and the poverty of my imagination in knowing how to deal with sibling conflict and family storms, I wondered whether my own insufficiencies affected my ability to give fully to my family.

I once read that our very incompleteness is the spaciousness into which we can welcome the flow of grace. We just have to let go of the guilt and self-recriminations that come with the territory of imperfection. Hard to do since motherhood is imperfection personified.

In retrospect, despite my restlessness and self-criticism, it was motherhood, and staying home with my three children for several years, that actually helped season me over time. From the sleepy daylight baby greetings, to the surprises arising from my children's home, school and friendship lives, to their attempts to defy the laws of nature in their athletic feats, everything unfolded in such a remarkable fashion. Participating in their growth struggles awakened the sense of my own value, for I never doubted I was needed in a primary way. I never doubted I loved them.

The months and years cascade down as children bounce up and out. They grow to become complex and fascinating people. Hellos are supplanted by good-byes as each child unintentionally walks away with your heart. Their independence is a sign of good parenting, but it is a parent's loss. It is another surrender for parents. This surrendering is to the world, which will take them from you. And the world can be so hard. This is where a mother must do a tightrope walk balancing faith with powerlessness. Her children's inexperienced adolescent and young adult choices can and often do have unintended consequences.

Every mother remembers a time when the fabric of unintended consequences is tugged or torn— mothers who witness their children hurt emotionally or physically, who witness burdens placed upon their children due to immature decisions, mothers who experience the terrible loss of a child to war, drug overdose, disease or fatal accident. As a mother, thankfully, I have not lost a child, but I remember times with my three children when the fabric was tugged, when I felt I bore their wounds.

I'll never forget when my youngest son Thomas was struck by a car on his bike at age 10 and lay on the street, in shock, with broken bones and lights of emergency vehicles flashing all around him. Or when my son Jesse at age seven was rushed to the hospital after falling and getting a deep gash right between the eyes. Or when my husband and I answered a call at one in the morning from a doctor in a distant city warning us that our college-age daughter might not pull through a medical emergency. Those were the times my body was no longer my own. Instead, my body was inhabited by the pain I carried for my children. Those were the times that required brute faith.

All humans carry an ideal of motherhood inside our hearts. We hold a longing for unconditional care from earliest childhood.

But what parent can really ever meet that ideal? And what child is ever fulfilled perfectly? Truth be told, we alternately hobble and sprint through family life. There's friction in being both a parent and a child, with lots of mistakes, anger, regrets and need for forgiveness. On the other hand, the graces of joy, laughter and gratitude are so pure and spontaneous they can't be measured.

While we live in the limitations of the real, the ideal is our deepest longing for God's perfect love. Faith reminds us that we are mothered by our God and by one another wherever we encounter a compassionate spirit. We are sometimes mothered by fathers, by aunts, uncles, grandparents, by siblings, teachers, true friends, by a favorite poet and a loving priest. Sometimes we can even mother ourselves when we remember that we each are God's beloved child.

In the Gospel of John, Jesus says, trust me—now and always. "Peace I leave with you; my peace I give to you. Not as the world gives do I give it to you. Do not let your hearts be troubled or afraid." This peace is a gift that mother-love always wishes upon her children. I can and do ask God to protect my adult children, to provide them with a guiding light, but there is no guarantee of a smooth journey.

I believe God is made of mother love. She dwells within our children and within each of us, celebrating and suffering with us every day. We belong to her—

this Mother God. And in this kinship, this trust, we can offer shelter for each other.

Reflections on Daughterhood

Not all of us are mothers or parents, but we are all sons and daughters of mothers. Some of us have lost our mothers. Some of our mothers still care for us, and for some, we are now caring for them in their later years. But as long as they are alive, mothers are the owners, the repositories and living archives of our early personal histories, histories that pre-date even our own infant and childhood memories.

Sometimes the boundary between my mother and me felt like a permeable membrane, with a force flowing both ways. My caring for my mom and her caring for me sometimes got mixed up over the years in a complex web of who was caring for whom, and who was protecting the other from hurt or disappointment.

But I've come to recognize that the way my mom and I carried each other internally had a lot to do with a deep sense of shared gender—our womanhood. As a daughter growing up, I was curious and connected, and so I watched my mom carefully. She taught me through her own personal sacrifices and vibrant spirit so much about loving a family.

During my college years, we had important talks about the women's movement and each of our identity struggles as women—mothers and daughters. Into my adulthood, I began to realize our lives had a lovely parallelism. We were both daughters of talented mothers. We were both wives of strong, ethical men and mothers of three children—two sons and one daughter. I really believe it's because of her that I will always be grateful I was born into a woman's body with a woman's soul.

Despite my mom's periodic struggles with depression during her life, her deepest currents seemed to flow out of her creative writing and the satisfactions she took in her family and relationships. I always loved observing her experience the pleasures of the intellect, reading, and the simple wonders of life—good food, the shared table, the beautiful earth, stimulating conversations, travel adventures, politics and art. I learned from her about hospitality, friendship, loyalty and fairness—values that I probably absorbed unconsciously in my childhood.

When I was 27 and she was 57, we wrote and published a book together, *Hostage To Heaven,* about my captivity in an authoritarian cult during the 1970's and my rescue through my parents' efforts. That mutual writing project brought much reconciliation and discovery. But especially in the last five years of her life, she helped me appreciate how deep is the mother-daughter connection. She is gone now and her passing was very hard. She was so attached to life, to people, to this earth—and I to her.

This is a poem I wrote to my Mom a few months before she died:

Time to Say Goodbye
When she is gone
It will rain in Oregon
I'm certain
Water will drip
From tiny pools
On leaves outside her window
Instead of from her eyes

Give me time
Before she goes
To collect her tears:
They are holy water –

For what was lived
Was graced

Her curled hands
Lay useless
Limp as lambskin gloves
Soft in her lap,
Her head
Nuzzles like a newborn
Into my neck

I must go now,
Time to say goodbye.

Before turning
Her eyes capture mine
Kiss me
And tell of the splendor
Of mother and child.

So many hellos
Along the way,
Loving
Before me and afar,
A pilgrim going
Home,
Every day emptying
Discarding, yielding
To her God
So wide and waiting.

© Barb Scharff

I was my mother's only daughter. The story of her last week of life reverberates through me. Mary Elizabeth Underwood, a Quaker, died at a Jewish nursing center in July 2009. In that graceful way that

God knits life and death across generations, my mother will forever be within me.

Our modern secular culture hyperactively drives us to outmaneuver death, but the experience of being a daughter, journeying beside and with my dying mother, conferred its own graces. For reasons unknown to me, I and my family were gifted with the invitation to enter into a sacred vigil with my mom during her last days.

My older brother Doug and I went to visit my mom on her last Sunday. I visited her every Sunday, but this one was different. Over the last five years she had become disabled and unable to speak clearly due to two serious strokes.

I needed to explain to Mom that hospice care would start the next day. I knew I must tell her she was dying. Some people sense their life is coming to an end, but my mother did not. She felt durable. When I told her that she wouldn't live long, she looked startled. I explained that she'd suffered a third major stroke and her swallowing reflex was completely disabled. She would no longer eat, drink or swallow. For years, she'd been clear that she didn't want a feeding tube to prolong her life. Without nourishment, her body would close down in a few days.

I said words I believe and hoped would console her—that we would take care of her, she wouldn't feel any pain and she would be in God's embrace. She was always the worrier, so I reassured her that she needn't feel anxious about her children or grandchildren. I remember I told her she was beautiful and she was created for eternity.

Doug and I stayed with her several hours remembering stories of our growing up. My mom just listened. We laughed, retelling quirky stories that constituted our family lore . . . like when Mom strapped Dad in his sleeping bag on top of our 1958 Ford station wagon to avoid bears on the ground while camping in Yosemite Valley. Or when Mom turned to me the night of the 120-mile-an-hour gusts during the Columbus Day storm—after we'd just moved to a bedroom community of Portland—and asked if it was always this windy in the suburbs. Or when Dad yelled at one of his adolescent kids, and we'd remind him that he was a pacifist!

Stories are the yeast of every family. With each story I gazed upon my mom, and thought about the length and depth, the complexity, generosity and rising of her life. A life is such a large thing. Hers was 88 years large.

From Sunday until Thursday, our family members—my two brothers, my sister-in-law, my husband and my mom's grandchildren—took turns sitting beside her. What took shape was a loving and patient vigil. We sat together with her, and we sat individually with her. We hummed songs she'd taught us long ago. Over and over we said thank you, I love you, and good-bye.

As the week progressed, I sensed a dissolving of boundaries between this moment and some incomprehensible future. Day by day her body diminished. Her head seemed so little, like a baby's head, easily cupped in my palm. Her spirit began the process of outgrowing her skin. A friend calls it the dilation of the spirit. She entered into that vulnerable space, that emptying where there was no volition on her part except to yield, where she could no longer protect herself mentally or physically from the inevitable cessation of her body's function. Through the crucible of grace, her extreme vulnerability met us, and broke our hearts.

By Wednesday, my mom entered a cocoon-like state. Her heart and lungs labored persistently with the force of life. We were witnessing the mystery of dying—how the vast passion of a discrete and marvelous human being yields to something as incomprehensible as eternity. How do we understand this mystery? It is no more knowable than the origin of the Cosmos or the Imagination that thought up an owl, an orchid or a newborn. We just believe.

All during the vigil, my brothers Doug, Jeff and I, my husband Gary and my sister-in-law Susanne felt an intense responsibility to stay with my mom, to accompany her to her last breath. We all thought she needed that from us. And in spite of our exhaustion, we were determined to stay with her.

Thursday night after my mom's life-long friends came and departed, our immediate family entered into a silent worship around her bed. We watched her chest rise and fall. We bowed in prayer. I longed for God to gather her in, to draw her into the fullness of love. During this deep silence, I experienced a peacefulness and hopefulness take over. I sensed that I could release her, that she didn't need me to deliver her to her crossing over. It seemed that my mom was already occupying that space where the divine breaks into life. I knew she was going home. And with that sense, I experienced the release of a great weight and responsibility. This was the moment she was entrusted to God.

Our hospice nurse advised us that many people need to make their final departure in solitude. Always the people-pleaser, my mom may have been holding on for us. So after five days of vigil at her bedside, our family left her and gathered for dinner Friday evening in a restaurant to take stock of the revelation and emotional work of the passing week.

After dinner, Susanne and I returned to sit at my mom's bedside. Upon entering the Jewish nursing center, we were told she had just passed away. It was just after sundown. We solemnly entered her room. An extraordinary stillness filled the space. The light from the western sky glowed orange and lit her utterly quiet body. My mom had taken her last breath in solitude, during Jewish prayer services.

"Death ends a life, but not a relationship," wrote my mom about her own mother's passing years earlier. I believe my mom is with God. She is also present with me—in the vibration of memory, in her poetry, published books and journals, her letters, photographs and hand-made jasper jewelry.

She was a loving and steadfast mom, and as a child I took in her love the way a leaf takes in sunshine, just naturally. But especially in the last five years of her life when she was coping with serious disabilities, she showed me there is a way to surrender to the things in life we can't control. She made it look ordinary, although I know it took bravery. She once said to me: "I've learned patience from people who have limitations. I've learned to accept my own impairments by living with others who are impaired."

At vigil's end, I learned that death cannot separate us from God's love. I learned how right it is to entrust our loved ones to God. It is not a choice but a reality. My mother took flight across a horizon unknown to me. My heart would have to catch up to its grace.

In the kinship of mothers and daughters, what we love is not to be fastened to this earth, but to be believed in. Love and good-bye. We will all someday vanish into the unknown. It is in this mystery that each one of us will someday be entrusted to God in the place where we started and the place where we end.

The End is the Beginning

If sonatas and dance,
Love making babies
Light
And all possibility
(my life)
Were to vanish from the earth
(in a twinkling or a blast,
And dark was the only tangible to last)
God would dream
Up
Water Music
And waltzes,
Rosemary,
Magentas
Babies and blue
Just as She must have done
The first time through.

© Barb Scharff

Suffering and Our Image of God

by Karen Nettler

WHEN I was 13, my Dad took a sabbatical from his ministry, and hired on as a fire lookout for the summer at one of the forest service towers in the central Oregon forest. We all went with him, living an idyllic life in a little one-room cabin with no running water, a wood stove for cooking, and a sleeping porch where the five of us children slept.

That life was shattered when my youngest brother, four-year-old Ted, a bright sunbeam of a boy, fell about 15 feet from the tower, hit his head on a concrete slab, and suffered a severe and permanent brain injury. In the immediate aftermath of the fall, our family was separated, kids parceled out to various places, while my parents spent their days by Ted's hospital bed in Portland.

I was with Ted when he fell. I was carrying a three year-old girl down the stairs from the top of the tower, with Ted following close behind. His foot caught, and there was no way for me to stop his fall. While I knew it was not my fault that I had been charged with taking two small children down from the tower, where the adults wanted to stay to watch a forest fire in the distance, still I began to wonder why this tragedy had happened.

One of the adults in the tower was the father of that little girl, and it was to their house that I went to stay for the first couple weeks after the fall. I was not close to him or his wife, and I had no one to talk to about my great grief and evolving guilt that somehow this accident was God's punishment. But, finally, on the way home from a church event with the father, I blurted out my fear that I was guilty and God was punishing me. I will never forget the father's silence as we drove, his silence as we got out of the car at his house, and his silence as we went into the house and he walked away. He had no words of reassurance for me. I can't imagine what was going through his mind, but what was going through mine was that apparently my guilt and fears were not groundless.

To my mother's great credit, she later made it clear to me that I was not to blame. But my image of God was profoundly shaped by Ted's accident, not only because God seemed so distant and detached from all of our suffering, but also because thousands of people were praying for Ted, to little avail. What would move the heart of God, if not the suffering of this beautiful little boy? So my experience of God was that, while he may love the whole world, he was distant and personally unengaged with me. It was up to me to pursue God and to seek to get his approval by believing and behaving right—something I never could successfully do, so I always felt that God was disappointed in me. My suffering, the suffering of the world, was apparently deserved, and it was only because of Jesus' death to cover my failures that God could tolerate me.

Out of many difficult and challenging circumstances in my life has come much healing, and the most profound and basic healing has come in my image of God. I now know without doubt that God pursues me with passion and longing for connection.

This healing journey has happened over many years, and continues to unfold. But as my experience of God changed, the issue of suffering became a dilemma, a disturbing question for me. How could God, who loved so deeply and felt our wounds so utterly, bear to allow suffering? I heard various explanations, none really satisfied, and suffering became a sticking point for me in my relationship with God.

Why suffering at all? And, is there meaning in suffering, does God cause it, and if so, for what purpose? As I worked through these questions, I found wisdom in a course I took on the subject of suffering, in books I read about how others had dealt with great suffering, and also in my own response to suffering as I experienced God in the midst of it. So, while I don't expect to fully comprehend why there is suffering, it does help me to have some grasp on what it is and is not.

First, what suffering is not: it is not a punishment for sin. It is not necessary to expiate for sin. It is not a means to win God's favor, let alone a means to exhaust his supposed wrath against us. It is not what was intended for creation. It is an intrusion into what was intended to be a mutually desired and life-fulfilling relationship that encompassed all of creation.

Suffering is not fully explained. While there are rational connections between evil and suffering, the deeper question of why evil and suffering exist at all remains something of a mystery. Suffering is also not the only reality. Beauty, love, and all that is good co-exist with it in a mysterious and wondrous way.

So, what is suffering? I've come to understand it as a result of the presence of evil, a clear sign of a creation gone awry. It is often random, and unrelated to what we did or did not do. But, because it is also the result of our own choices, suffering is often a feeling of shame for our actions, and tragically, often an experience of shame for who we are.

Suffering is the experience of existential pain resulting from our sense of alienation from God and ourselves. We are stuck with it, as an unavoidable aspect of our humanity. So, suffering is also the dis-ease resulting from living with an awareness of what was meant to be, while experiencing a world that is unjust and full of pain. But, when we surrender to that reality, we are more fully alive and present to the world, and can choose to respond in a life-giving way. Suffering is therefore, paradoxically, a way of experiencing life at its deepest level.

Nothing I've read over the years about suffering leads me to conclude that suffering was introduced into our experience for a purpose. It comes as a natural consequence of evil, but it also comes nonsensically. For my brother Ted, the lights went dim for him at the age of four; the God-breathed dreams and desires thwarted for him from that time on. His ongoing suffering is nothing other than obscene to me. But what I have come to understand is that suffering is not meaningless. It does produce something, depending on how we respond. Given that suffering is, there is meaning to be found.

Suffering, fully embraced and experienced, is where we are most ourselves, and where we are most connected with a wounded world. We long for connection, yet are often afraid to make ourselves vulnerable. Suffering can break through the barriers, and move us to compassion for our common wounds. Suffering can pare away the artificial, and bring us home to ourselves and God. A wise person once said that God is waiting for us all to weep so that the world can be transformed. Blessed are those who weep, for their tears will be wiped away. We must first weep in order to experience the consolation.

Most of all, suffering is where God connects with us, where God joins the human experience. Though it is a lonely road to be suffering, because no one can truly bear it for us, it is where we are invited to most deeply experience God's suffusing love for us.

Our understanding of suffering is so much informed by our own experience, but suffering has meaning beyond our own experience of it. It is mystery how that may be, but the faith that it is so gives meaning, though the actual result may not be known in this life. Suffering does not have the last word; not ultimately, and also not in the here and now. Evil is exposed by our suffering fully our humanity, not being defeated by it, and finding life, joy, beauty even in the midst of darkness.

Finally, suffering is not the point of our existence. Relationship with God is. Suffering, in a way, becomes the greatest struggle toward relationship. If God desires suffering, he can't be trusted. So suffering becomes a leap of faith, a surrendering to Divine purpose while not fully understanding. Being in relationship with God means I'm suspending my questions to be with him. Not because the questions go away, but because I need to be held by God in my suffering.

So, the most primal truth I've come to in my journey about suffering is that I am not alone. I already knew that on many deep and trustworthy levels, but somehow, when it came to suffering, I had a go-it-alone framework. Not anymore. Knowing I am never abandoned in my deepest sufferings—to the contrary, it is where God meets me most fully in the suffering of Jesus—does not answer the question of why there is suffering, but it mutes the questions. Experiencing "never alone" does not necessarily relieve the suffering. But it casts it in a new light, so that I see and know it differently. It also somehow sanctifies it—making the humanity of it all holy, transcendent. The ultimate "here's the plan" that explains the necessity of suffering? That doesn't exist. It doesn't need to, when the suffering is embraced as what makes us fully human, containing somehow both human and divine. That we dare to carry and be present to that tension and therefore be with suffering, is where we most experience one-ness with the One we most desire, which by divine paradox, is the place of deep joy.

Home In God's Hands

by Marie Goretti Abijuru
as told to Maureen Hovenkotter

*Peace I leave with you, My peace I give to you;
not as the world gives do I give to you. Let not
your heart be troubled, neither let it be afraid.
– John 14:27*

IMAGINE WAKING UP in a strange apartment, in an unfamiliar city in a country halfway around the world from everything you have ever known. You don't know where anything is, you don't understand the culture, and you don't even know the language. Your community, your family, your friends are thousands of miles away; your husband, who died more than a year earlier, is buried back home. All you have are your three young children and your faith. You alone are responsible for making this new place home and helping your children settle into a completely new life.

Seven years ago that is where I found myself. It is where refugee and immigrant families often find themselves: escaping the horrors of violence or oppression but mystified and lost, having to start over again almost as completely as if they had just been born. It was never a situation I expected to find myself in, not in my wildest dreams.

My life began innocently enough as the first child of a Catholic couple who had been married for 20 years and all but given up hope for having children. My parents were so pleased to finally be blessed by a child, they bestowed on me a name that means "heavenly" or "of heaven." Three years after I was born, my brother arrived. It was a wonderful childhood. I grew up as an adored and beloved miracle, surrounded by family and friends who considered me as a blessing. I was secure in the knowledge that I was loved and in my understanding of the kind of life my future held. Of course, none of us ever knows what life has in store for us.

Life in our small village in the mountains of Rwanda was good, but simple. We had no electricity, no in-house plumbing. We walked everywhere; cars were only for the very rich people. I was raised in a strong faith; we went to Mass regularly and prayed together every day. My father was a teacher, my father's father—my grandfather—was also a teacher and taught me first grade.

Rwanda is a beautiful country, very green with many trees. Oregon reminds me of my homeland very much. The winters are very cold in the north, there are many mountains and hills, and it rains a lot, which also reminds me of Oregon.

Because Rwanda is a small country, the people take full advantage of the limited space. There are very few empty places. Citizens own most of the land; there is very little government-owned land beyond a few very large forests and parks. People live in the many small villages. Each extended family has a plot of land on which they grow vegetables and other plants around their houses.

Families divide off pieces of land for each son as he reaches adulthood and prepares to marry. Before they marry, the young men have to build a house on their piece of land to bring their wife home to. Adult children cannot live with their parents once they are married, and there are no houses for rent in the villages. Rwanda is a patriarchal society. Daughters stay home with their families until they get married. In the rare cases of divorce, the children belong to the father's family.

Early in 1994 I married Felicien Gashongore, and I worked for Caritas Rwanda while my husband attended IAMSEA University. Our son Valentin was born later that year and our life was good.

In spite of my good life and my sense of security, I knew there were troubles in my country. Conflict between the two main tribes of Rwanda—the Tutsi and the Hutu—had rocked the country for decades and thousands of people had died.

In the early 1990s conflict escalated in Rwanda. In 1991 the Rwandan Patriotic Front, mainly made up of expatriated or exiled Tutsis who had left the country when the Hutus gained power, invaded the country and the war broke out.

Life had become very dangerous in Rwanda, but it was about to become a nightmare. On April 6, 1994, President Juvenal Habyarimana's plane was shot down. The assassination led to a brutal wave of killing known as the Rwandan Genocide which, within a three-month period, left between 500,000 and 1,000,000 Tutsis and moderate Hutus dead.

Terrible things were happening in my country. So many people were dying. Fortunately my family was spared. Thanks be to God!

Felicien was in his last year at the University, studying statistics and economics. Because of the conflict, the school was closed and the students were transferred to ENSEA, the similar University in Ivory Coast. In order to finish his degree, he moved to the Ivory Coast in February, 1995. I followed with Valentin in July, 1996, after my husband graduated.

Felicien and I set about building a new life in the Ivory Coast where the government had been stable for many years—since its independence from France in 1960—under President Felix Houphouet-Boigny. The stability and safe environment fostered a strong, healthy economy and life again looked promising.

Felicien and I both found good jobs. I did some accounting and clerical work in a clinic; he worked as a consultant. We joined a Catholic church, and soon our family grew to include another son and a daughter (Valois and Vanessa). Our children were baptized in this new faith community. We had many friends, a good home and faith community in which to raise our three children. We had all that we needed. Life was good.

We were very involved in our church. We attended Mass regularly, participated in novenas, and retreats. I joined a Divine Mercy prayer group at St. Elisabeth Church, and our group prayed for churches, priests, peace and for the safety in the whole world where violence was occurring. During this time I grew very close to God and the Virgin Mary, deepening my faith and compassion. I think this was the beginning of a very deep relationship with God that carried me through the many challenges that lay ahead of me. On

May 22, 2004, I was consecrated to the Virgin Mary. In that ceremony, I realized how much I needed my faith to be renewed.

Although Ivory Coast had been stable under one leader for many years, there had been a push to have democratic elections before we arrived. At first this had no effect, but by late 1999 political conflicts had escalated and resulted in a coup on Christmas Day. Things were beginning to fall apart politically in Ivory Coast and violence ensued even where we had thought we were safe from it.

In a wave of violence, my husband was attacked one night while walking home from work. Someone wielding a machete attempted to slash his throat but only succeeded in cutting his face and hand savagely when he put an arm up to protect himself. Although he recovered from the injury and continued to work for more than two years, the injury and inadequate medical care had left him weakened. In July of 2003, returning from work in Senegal, he fell seriously ill. He never recovered and on July 27, I was with him in the hospital when he died. I wept for more than half an hour, bereft and lost. "What do I do? How can I survive without you?" I kept asking.

Then suddenly I heard an answer to my pleas: *Stop this crying, now. You will be okay. You can do this.*

I knew God was there with me in my loss and was able to immediately accept it. I stopped crying and began singing God's praises. Thanks to my friend Domitille who joined me in that journey of acceptance and trust.

The workers and other people who were in the hospital were upset with me. My husband had just died. I was supposed to be overcome with grief and here I was, singing. I think maybe they thought I was losing my mind. But I knew God had some purpose and that God would be with me in this journey.

After Felicien's death, my father asked me if I should come back to Rwanda and bring the children to be with our family. I told him I had a job, I had friends and a faith community in Ivory Coast. I reminded him that he had been with his wife, my mother, for 20 years before my brother and I had come along. I now had my own life and even though my husband was no longer here to help me, I could take care of my children and continue to live my life. My father reluctantly agreed.

After my husband died, I had decided to emigrate to Europe. However, at one point someone suggested I consider going to the United States instead. *Why would I want to go there*, I asked myself. *I don't know anyone. I can't even speak the language.* But again, just as I had felt other times, I sensed God's presences and believed this was something I was supposed to do. I applied and within ten months on a day late in the summer of 2004 I found myself with my children in a plane on the way to the United States.

Often the United Nations High Commission for Refugees, the international agency that helps settle refugees, tries to place people in areas in which they have family or friends, but we knew no one in the U.S. Refugees are sponsored and initially supported by local agencies and placed within the region the agency serves. The agency that had been selected to help me and my family was Catholic Charities' Refugee Resettlement program in Portland. At first I thought it was Portland, Maine, and since I had friends in Canada, I thought perhaps I would be close to them. We changed plane in Paris and then flew onward to Chicago where my children and I boarded the plane traveling to Oregon.

On September 1, 2004, a completely new and unfamiliar life began for my children and me. I later learned that there were immigrants from Rwanda who had been here for many years, I didn't know that then, and I felt very much alone. I received a first call from a Rwandese family who lives here in Portland after two months. I was so excited.

Before refugees arrive, the sponsoring agency secures apartments for them to begin their new life and provides rent payments for the first eight months. Refugees receive work permits upon arriving in the U.S., and their sponsoring agency helps them get official identification, apply for their social security cards, open bank accounts, set up telephones, medical screenings, and obtain immunizations for children so they can go to school. They help refugees register their children in school; take the family to Department of Human Services to apply for food stamps and to get medical insurance.

There are many new things to learn about, especially for people who have been living in very poor villages and refugee camps who may not even know about basic sanitation, plumbing or electricity. Most of the time refugees are also dealing with a language barrier, knowing little, if any, English. Some people don't even know how to write their own names, and most really don't know anything about the culture and about living in America.

Here in Portland it is the Immigrant and Refugee Community Organization (IRCO) that helps the new refugees and immigrants become acculturated and qualify to receive continued benefits as long as necessary to get established. IRCO offers English classes and, if refugees already speak English, helps them try to find work immediately. They issue bus passes for up to five months and train people on how to use mass transit and how to read maps of the city so they can get around. They assign new refugees and immigrants a job coach to help them find work and provide career coaching. IRCO helps refugees for up to five years living in U.S.

For me, as for many refugees and immigrants, the biggest barrier was language. French was the official language of both Rwanda and Ivory Coast. While I had studied English in school, as did some students in my country, it was only for a short time and was many years ago. Some people volunteer to teach English language to the refugees and immigrants in their homes. I give thanks for Pat Dutmers and Sarah Woolley who was assigned to teach me at home, and became the best friends of mine.

After I was a bit more comfortable with the English language, I began looking for work but found it difficult to find a job. I received training in customer service, retail management, computers and medical records. Working with computers came very easy to me, but I was more challenged by jobs in which I had to communicate with people. I continually worried about how I could improve my listening and language skills. I was afraid if the people called I wouldn't be able to talk to them. I loved the experience but wondered how I could successfully work in an office and take calls from a variety of people.

I did internships at the library for six months, at Legacy Good Samaritan Hospital for three months and at the Oregon Health Sciences University. I worked for another three months at the Oregon Employment Department, all the while trying to go to school and take care of my family. I worked hard, trying to fit into this society and use my skills and experiences. These internships helped give me training and job experience, but they did not pay anything.

I worried about having enough money to take care of my children. I thought about doing housekeeping but knew that would not get me to my goal of working in the field of business and accounting, which I loved. At least for the time being I preferred to live on the $617 I received in assistance and learn office work. That, at least, was closer to my dream.

What I really wanted to do was go to college to prepare for a career that would help me provide well for my family. But because I still had small children at home, I couldn't afford to not work and pay for daycare. If I refused to look for a job I wouldn't get help paying for daycare. For a time I went to school while doing the internships. Then I finally knew that I really needed to have more income so I began working for Nike while still trying to take classes.

When I first arrived in Portland, I had to find someone to take care of my children. I was so blessed to find a wonderful childcare provider named Rhonda Evans who watched them for four years. It was almost like having my mother with me. She came to our apartment to pick the children up, took the older ones to school, made sure they were taken care of on weekends and evenings while I was working. She was a wonderful help and allowed me to work and go to school without worrying about my children.

It finally proved to be too difficult for me to work full time and go to school while being a single parent of small children. After five months I knew I would have to let go of something. I didn't feel I was doing a very good job being a mother; I wasn't able to attend church because I was working on weekends, which was very difficult for me. I finally asked myself what I was doing. Did I come to the U.S. to try to become wealthy? This was not a life I was comfortable with, always working or studying. I began looking for another job.

By then Vanessa was going to preschool, and I heard that they were looking for a part-time teacher's assistant in the Head Start program. I applied and was hired. I left Nike and felt that the part-time job would allow me to go to school full time. The following summer when the school closed, I began to volunteer at IRCO to keep me busy. In July they asked me to take a temporary paid job to fill in while one of the employees was on sick leave. I agreed to work for IRCO until preschool started again in September, but by September she was not yet able to return to work. I liked the work at IRCO but knew I would lose the job once the other employee was able to come back so it was hard to give up the Head Start job. IRCO talked me into staying. She was finally able to come back to work; IRCO offered me a full time position in December 2007. I couldn't believe that I had a full time job in an office, especially where I serve the refugees and immigrants. But I had to drop out of school and put my dream of getting a degree in business or accounting on hold. It is hard for me to work full time, take care of my children, and go to school.

One of the greatest gifts I discovered shortly after arriving in Portland came as I was riding the bus down Powell Boulevard. I looked out the window and saw a Catholic church. I didn't know where any Catholic churches were. Not having a church where

I could go and take my children to worship on Sundays was a huge loss to me, so seeing this large white church with children playing on the playground seemed like a beacon of hope to me. I will never forget the first Sunday we visited St. Ignatius together with my neighbor from Sudan and his family. I was welcomed, and began taking my children there. St. Ignatius has been our faith community ever since that day. I never miss Mass. Even when I didn't know what they were saying, it was enough that I was there to pray. Facing Jesus on the cross and the Virgin Mary and sharing Eucharist means so much to me. I am now very glad to be a member of St. Ignatius parish, and fully participate in Mass as I wanted.

When my children were accepted into the school, I was so happy. I believe that God heard and answered my prayers. Even when they grow up and change, as they choose their own lives, something will stay with them from the years they were in Catholic school and went to church.

My faith is something that makes me stronger, because without that, living as a single mother in this country would have been too difficult. I rely on God, and I trust that God will help. Now I have a lot of friends and many of those friends come from my church. Although I have no parents or brothers and sisters here in this country, I feel like I have a big family. My children and I were in a car accident recently. Within five minutes of calling the school to let them know, the principal was by our side. Everyone at church was praying for us and offering to help us. This is a gift I can't measure. I don't have to worry about what is going to happen tomorrow or in the future. I am in good hands, I am in God's hands, and no one can ever take that feeling of safety and peace away from me. I am the witness of a thousand miracles in my life, and I learned the good lesson in the difficult moment. Thanks be to God!

To Turn and to Fly with Love

by Cheryl Rohret

IT'S EASTER morning, and it's my birthday. Someone on Facebook sends me a note telling me the last time Easter was on this day was in 1859. An auspicious occurrence, I tell myself as I get ready for day. But I knew that already. It's Easter Sunday, my birthday, and this butterfly is emerging from her cocoon—again. Or, to use another of my favorite metaphors, I'm ready for another turn on the labyrinth of my life

Two hours later, I put on the bunny ears headband I found at our rummage sale and step up to greet my congregation.

"Happy Easter!" I proclaim.

"Hoppy Easter!" someone says back. And we're off! It's going to be a great day of celebration at Unity Spiritual Life Center.

Labyrinths and butterflies are recurring metaphors in my life. Each describes in a different way what it means to move through the inevitable changes life brings. How can I find the center that holds? What will it take for me to emerge into the fullness of who I am? I like that the labyrinth has me walking to ground myself, while the butterfly gives me an image of flying free with Spirit. I wouldn't want one without the other. Both are part of what it means to be human . . . or, as we like to say in Unity, to be "spiritual beings having a human experience."

I smile as I write this, thinking to myself, "You've come a long way, Baby, from your traditional Presbyterian roots!"

I was raised a P.K. (Preacher's Kid), the third of four daughters born to Dick and Mary Betty Johnson. My father was a Presbyterian minister who started a new church in 1954 in a suburb south of Seattle. By the time I got to high school, Dad had left the pastorate and become the first hospital chaplain at Swedish Hospital in Seattle. We had many rich traditions when I was growing up, in our family and in the faith communities that were part of our life. I knew about Sunday morning orders of worship, going to Sunday School before the worship service, memorizing Bible verses, taking the knot out of my handkerchief to put my offering in the plate each week. I sang lively gospel songs and stately hymns. I knew the Lord's Prayer and the Apostles' Creed by heart. I felt honored to go through the communicants' class to become a member at age 11 so I could take communion once a quarter. I loved church. In fact, I used to sneak over to the sanctuary and play preacher until the custodian found me one day and scolded me.

In 1980, I became a Presbyterian minister myself. When I started my ministerial training, many Protestant churches were in the midst of a liturgical renewal, bringing back some of the ancient symbolism and ritual that had been thrown out in the Reformation. I loved all the seasons of the church year with their colors and how they told the story of Jesus' life and ministry. I loved the opening words of the Communion service: "The Lord be with you . . . And also with you." I loved that when I went to a Roman Catholic service, I could sing or say much of the liturgy right along with the rest of the congregation.

(Except for that "I am not worthy" part. I never understood that.)

In 1988, I moved to Central Washington as the minister of Naches Presbyterian Church in the small town of Naches, 14 miles west of Yakima. We celebrated all the seasons of the church year. We shared communion once a month. I baptized and married and buried, preached many sermons about God's love meant to shine through us, introduced contemporary music at the beginning of our services, and loved the people. Our little church grew from 30 to 90 in worship. I also met and married Vic, who joined right in every Sunday after going to Mass at the Catholic Church. I got to confirm my son, Evan. It was, in many ways, a wonderful time of ministry.

It was wonderful, except for one thing: As time went on, I found I didn't believe the tenets of the Apostles' Creed anymore. I also couldn't bear the determination of the Presbytery of Central Washington (composed of ministers and elders from the churches in our area) to exclude and condemn people on the basis of their gender preference. When I left the Naches congregation in 1997, it was because I no longer felt like I belonged to the Presbyterian Church I had signed on with in 1980. The Church had taken steps backward into a conservatism that did not fit for me.

My last Sunday to preach at Naches Presbyterian Church was one week shy of the nine-year anniversary of my arrival there. The sermon that day was "We Are a New Creation." I shared with tears and laughter some of the many ways God had brought new life to all of us during our time together. Then at the very end of the sermon I took off my pastor's robe to reveal a gold sequined butterfly vest over my red dress. The congregation rose to their feet in a standing ovation.

That butterfly was a symbol to them, and to me, of hope for new life. I needed it as much as they did.

It was much the same with the labyrinth. I stepped onto my first one in 1995. It wasn't the most beautiful one I've ever walked. A colleague in ministry had made it out of a huge blue tarp with the lines drawn with black permanent marker. The surroundings were certainly not mystical or inspiring. The tarp was laid out that day in a church gymnasium. There were no candles lit or lovely music playing. The only sound was the shuffling of seventy pairs of women's stocking feet moving on tarp—a tarp that got big, deep wrinkles in it the longer we walked. We had to be careful that our toes wouldn't get tripped up in those wrinkles. The average age of those walking that day was 65-70 years old. This was a gathering of Presbyterian Women of Central Washington Presbytery, and we were learning about different ways of praying.

I stepped up to the beginning of the path where the Rev. Jim Caulkins held the space for us, having us wait until the person ahead had gone around the first big curve before we each began walking. He had assured us that a labyrinth was not a maze. There were no tricks or dead ends. If we followed the path, we would reach the center. I wasn't so sure. All those lines on the tarp made no sense from where I was standing. I'd never in my life seen a labyrinth before. I found it a bit intimidating. But I was a leader and a minister, just like Jim. I needed to be brave and model willingness to try new things. Jim nodded at me, and I began to walk.

Maybe you think I'm going to tell you that lights came on, voices spoke, and I was brushed by angels' wings on that walk. Actually, I'm still waiting for any of those things to happen to me when I walk a labyrinth. It wasn't that kind of experience for me.

What drew me into that first labyrinth experience were the metaphors, the glorious metaphors that just wouldn't stop.

I started on the path and within one or two turns, it looked like I would reach the center, my destination. "That was easy," I thought. But, lo and behold, another couple of turns and I found myself suddenly out on the far edges of the path. *"Well, haven't I done that before in my life?"* I remember thinking to myself.

Walking with so many others on the path, I noticed how sometimes I would be walking side by side with a person, only to have us each come to a new turn and go off in totally different directions. Some people kept showing up in my line of sight again and again, until we had to begin smiling at each other as we passed—fellow pilgrims on the journey. There were times when we all seemed to clump together in one quadrant, then just as quickly we seemed to scatter all over the path.

When at last I arrived at the center, I found myself just needing to stop and celebrate with an internal *"Yippee! I made it!"* But then I realized that was only half of the walk. There was still the journey of re-tracing my steps on the same path to go out.

Finally I wound my way through to the end, which was also the beginning. I stepped off the path and off the tarp. Then I just kept walking around the outside perimeter of this amazing circle of meaning, shaking my head in wonder and going, "Wow!"

I didn't know it then, but that day I began my discovery of a way to begin to make sense out of all the twists and turns in my life. Am I really on a path that is taking me to the center, to God, if I faithfully follow it? Can I trust that if I keep putting one foot in front of the other in my life, it will lead me somewhere I want to go? And what happens when I leave the center and the defined path and walk back into ordinary life? Deep within my soul, this archetypal image was raising as many questions as it was answering. I loved it! The adventure of starting out on a path I didn't know, the sense of accomplishment in walking the whole way in and out . . . somehow the experience felt familiar, even in its newness to me that day. Yes, I'd been this way before.

I floated without a spiritual community for eight years after leaving Naches. It seemed I was on a quest to find the real Cheryl. Who am I if I am not the pastor of a church? What is my purpose, God? Why am I here? At times I grew weary of the search and at other times I felt exhilarated by it. I took Interim Ministry training and became an interim minister. No, I realized, that wasn't what I wanted to do with my life. I took a two-year course in spiritual formation called "Listening with the Spirit" and became a certified spiritual director. I loved doing that, but people weren't rushing to me for spiritual direction. I learned more about labyrinths and was trained by Dr. Lauren Artress to be a labyrinth facilitator. I even bought a 36-foot portable canvas labyrinth from another labyrinth facilitator and offered labyrinth walks every month in Yakima for a full year. Again, not a big response to what I was offering.

About a year and a half after leaving Naches, I attended a clergy retreat and was introduced to Celtic Christianity. It was love at first hearing. My heart resonated with the ancient Celts' ability to see God present in all things, with no arbitrary division between the sacred and the ordinary. God was in everything. They honored men and women as equally able to lead and work together for the good of the whole community. They weren't afraid of mystery, speaking of "thin places" where the veil between heaven and earth is very thin, permeable. And they believed we were all born blessed and beautiful, not condemned from the get-go by original sin. Contrasting all of this with the Roman Christian tradition (of which my Presbyterian heritage was a part), I finally understood why I had never quite felt like I belonged. It seemed I had been a Celtic Christian all along, living in a Roman world!

Though I didn't realize it at the time, these various strands of my experience and learning began to come together when I got acquainted with the new minister at Unity Spiritual Life Center in Yakima. Rev. Sandra and I became prayer partners.

One day, as I described this Celtic connection I felt, Sandra said to me, "Well, you know, Cheryl, that's a lot like what Unity believes."

I thought that was interesting, but didn't go any further with it. After all, I was born and raised Presbyterian. With Sandra's encouragement, however, Unity was the first place I spoke about my love of Celtic spirituality. My talk was well received, and I remember thinking, *"Wow, they really seem to get me . . ."*

In November of 2004, Sandra received a call to serve another Unity congregation. She asked me to speak the first two Sundays after she left. Since they knew me, she figured this would provide some comfort for the congregation. One of those Sundays, I shared a powerful story about love revealed one Christmas to a hurting family in the middle of a harsh winter. I felt like the congregation and I really connected as I told this story.

A week later, I was sitting with a friend who had been there. Charlotte told me she had had a spiritual experience as I spoke, seeing an image of me glowing as I stood in a perfectly-fitted white robe with golden threads.

She said, "What if Unity could be the place where you do your ministry?"

As I told her later, when she asked me that, something leapt within me. A spark of possibility was ignited and began to take shape as an idea in my mind. We call this conversation our Mary and Elizabeth experience, for when Mary, the mother of Jesus, came to tell her cousin Elizabeth that she was with child, Elizabeth, who was also pregnant, told her that the child within her leapt for joy at the news. This sacred moment with my friend is one that we re-visit often. It was the spark that set me on the path to become a Unity minister—another turn on the labyrinth of my life.

Six-and-a-half years later, I am now an ordained Unity minister. This woman who swore she would never do congregational ministry again is no longer burned out, is maybe a bit wiser (OK, a LOT wiser!), and is definitely having more fun as a minister. I have reclaimed my original call to ministry.

What is this call to ministry all about? For me, it is and always has been about being a "Good News Bearer." The Love and Goodness that permeate the universe are palpable to me. Even in the darkest moments of my life when I could not see the Light, the power of faith was alive in me and carried me through. When words failed me, somehow the Presence and Power of God stayed with me, and I was given what was needed to move through the darkness back into the light. This is what I want to share with others in my ministry and my life: "The light shines in the darkness, and the darkness did not overcome it." (John 1:5) To be a Good News Bearer is to let the light of Christ shine from me, not only to give light for myself but to light the way for others—to reflect back to them the light of Christ that is already shining in them.

The turns on the path keep coming. As of this writing, I am separated from my husband of 21 years. It isn't easy, especially doing life in front of a whole congregation. Thankfully, one of the things I have learned along the way is that the more real I am, the more that allows others to be real, too. And real life is not always neat and tidy with storybook endings.

Still, today is Easter and my birthday. The butterfly tattoo I bravely had inscribed on my ankle several years ago is my constant reminder that new life emerges when I risk opening and stepping away from my safe cocoon. The breath of God will be there to dry my wings and my tears, setting me free to fly once more with Love.

Mission Country

by Katie Hennessy

***Woman, behold, your son. . . . Behold your
Mother.** – **(John 19:26, 27)***

BENT AROUND the turn of this century, I spent a
potent portion of my social work career at a small
agency with a mission to serve women and children
impacted by HIV and AIDS. At that time little was
known about the "lived experience" of women,
children and families affected by the stigmatizing, life-
threatening, and often life-ending, disease.

My role was outreach worker in six different,
mostly rural counties. I visited homes, shelters,
prisons, jails and sometimes—very sad times—
hospitals. In doing so, *my* lived experience became
one of witnessing losses of health, employment,
housing, family and family support, esteem, security
and the remaining shreds of dignity in lives already so
drained of all the above, if there really had been any of
these to start. In larger measure, I was also able to
bear witness to strength and courage, faith, love and
the enviable wealth of community when these women
and their kids would find one another.

I arrived into the lives of those with HIV as an
assumed ally. This contrasted sharply with the role I
filled at the start of my career. In the early 80s I

served a necessary-yet-imposing child welfare function in a tough, east coast neighborhood. At 22 years old, I was clearly the enemy sent to judge and flash power—the poster child of a system and culture mostly clueless during those years. Sixteen years later I attempted to stand against poverty and shame with those I endeavored to stand alongside. I was one to whom stressed women-mothers could confide lifetimes of forced sex, sex exchanged for survival, the ruins of one-night stands, drug use, violence, feelings of betrayal or just plain chronic chaos. To be clear, not all women and families who live with HIV and AIDS share these stories in common—maybe not even most; but back then, many who asked for our involvement, did.

One of the hardest parts of a long career in social work is that much of what one sees, hears, experiences—the stuff of nocturnal tossing and turning and tearful drives home—are things about which she cannot speak, especially to those closest to her. So it was in those years. I spent long, lonely miles in reflections of days' events: the two-room malodorous apartment claimed as home by 24 family members, the hole in a residential ceiling/roof so gaping that one could not distinguish where the sky ended and the living room began, the silver trailer pocketing several recently-released corrected right outside the prison gate—human beings with no place else to go, no idea of what to do next.

And always, there were the children.

One Holy Week during those years I contemplated one family's story as I concentrated on the Crucifix and some of the last words Jesus said: "When Jesus saw his Mother and the disciple there whom he loved, he said to his Mother, 'Woman, behold, your son.' Then he said to the disciple, 'Behold your Mother.'" (John 19:26, 27).

50

She was a very young mother with AIDS and several children. Along with the treasure-containing backpacks each carried everywhere the family went, they all possessed a never-ending commitment of love and care for one another. This abiding, devoted love remained in the face of homelessness and chronic illness, among other losses and obstacles. Several factors—not the least of these poverty and pain—eventually combined and collapsed in on the mother's ability to directly care for her kids, and as a result they were separated from one another. The children went to live with relatives in another part of the state, and the future of all in the family was unsure. She, their mother, struggled intensely with what she articulated as the greatest loss of all.

Shortly after the removal of those kids I drove out to see them, to see how they were doing. Generally speaking, it started out as nice visit. I happened to arrive at the same time some new helping professionals in their lives arrived, and so I was able to hear reports of how they were doing in school and about new activities in which they were involved. On the face of things, all seemed okay. But as the visit went on, I experienced a growing palpable sense of unspoken uncertainty, grief and loss that made the whole encounter hard to endure. Because there were several new people there, I had a hunch I shouldn't dive too deeply into these intuited feelings conversationally. And so eventually, we said our good-byes, and I walked out the front door. As I was walking to my car to head back home, *the woman's only son followed me and called me by name.*

I turned around and went back to him.

Looking up at me he said, "What's going to happen to us?"

That was the question of that decade for me because, in a very broad but deep sense, I often wondered what was going to happen to many of those kids and their mothers I met and talked to, county after county. Many, many families' struggles mirrored this exact scenario. Many inquired, "What is going to happen to us?"

Inasmuch as I felt on the spot, I was also relieved by the question because it had the potential to be the first real exchange of the day, at least for me. But I realized when I looked into his beautiful little eyes as he was asking this question that I was seeing far more than wonder; I was seeing raw sorrow.

I got closer to him, and he continued, "I mean I love my family here and its good here and everything but . . ."

". . . but you miss your mom," I said.

And he looked down and nodded yes, and then he said, "Someday I want to be with her again."

That same human uncertainty, that insecurity about personal future mixed with grief, loss, sadness, despair and especially that question "what is going to happen to us" is what I believe Jesus is speaking to in this final bequest in these last words.

Clearly those hours on the cross were traumatic hours. In Jesus' story as told by John, this statement is immediately preceded by the awful event of Jesus' garments being torn into four parts, one for each of the soldiers doing the tearing, and then the casting of lots for the tunic which could not be evenly divided.

For those standing by, and standing by Jesus, this had to be an event that seemed metaphoric of the ripping and tearing of the ministry and the mission itself. Casting lots for his clothes: who knew that things would get so creepy? If we were standing by, and standing by Jesus, would we not wonder what is to happen to us? Even if the wonder or question was never articulated, there seems to have been a need for

Jesus to make clear what he wanted of those who loved him.

At the foot of the cross was Mary the Mother of Jesus, the one who shared so completely in his joyful moments, his moments of challenge, and now in his dying. She was the one who had witnessed his first small steps as a little baby and those first big steps when she encouraged him to begin his ministry at the wedding feast at Cana.

Here too, is the one whom Jesus loved and trusted enough to take care of his Mother whom he loved very deeply. Both knew that there could be no substitute for Jesus in their lives, just as my little friend understood that no one could take the place of his mother. In a very personal way, Jesus was "closing shop," making sure his Mother and friend were looked after. But there was also a much deeper bequest that Jesus was making.

Many of the phrases we give meaning to on Good Friday seem to be represented by the vertical axis of the cross, the relationship with the Abba Father. This phrase, however, seems to have to do more with the horizontal, our relationship with the Mother of our Jesus and our relationships with one another through that Jesus.

In the commentaries written about these final statements, there is a universal understanding that one of the things Jesus is doing when he says this is pairing his Mother with us and us with his Mother. She becomes our Mother, our instructive parent who tells us as she told those at Cana: "Do whatever he tells you." The easiest way for me to explain who Mary has become for me, a Roman Catholic woman in the 21st century, is to share an image.

One of the first things I do when I come into St. Ignatius Church, my parish church for the last 25 years, is to check to see if the Crucifix spotlights are on. This is not only because I believe that Jesus' death on the cross is central in our understanding of our faith, but because the lights create a shadow behind the Crucifix I have prayed with for years.

It is a shadow that resembles a woman to me, a woman who is the Mother of Jesus. As the years have gone by, the image has become replete with the many dimensions of whom I believe Mary is and more recently, whom I believe we are all called to be.

It is precisely because it is a shadow, a shadow with very little crisp definition or ego, that it means so much to me. It reveals to me how little we know about the person of Mary in anything that is written about her, but what we do know is what's important. We know that she was behind Jesus in everything he did, including death on the cross. We know that she was close to him, so close to him that the sword that would pierce Jesus would pierce her as well, as prophetic Simeon said it would. And we know that with her yes, her "Let it be done according to your word," she lived her life in a constant surrender and a faithfulness that has her arms outstretched as in that shadow, as if to say, "and even this, my pain, my sorrow, my only son—I offer up to you."

To be close enough to that cross, to be in that shadow, is the point. To be proximal enough to experience scrutiny and pain with Him and with each other is the point. To be in deep conversation with our God, in authentic anger when it's there and in true forgiveness and peace when they arrive, is the point. To lack crisp definition and ego is the point. To work and pray more for justice, to take risks on behalf of each other enough to carry the very human fear of what will happen to us, to enter into and be transformed by what my own earthly mother called the "mission country" all around us and in us—it is all the point.

54

The disciple whom Jesus loved is also close enough to be in that shadow. If we believe that we are all "the disciple whom Jesus loved" and loves, it further underscores that we are all called to the foot of that cross, to be in that shadow.

Inasmuch as I believe that these words are about our Mother and our Church, I also believe that Jesus is speaking to Mary "the Woman" and all that this construction means, with her 30-plus years' experience as the first disciple, and to us as disciples as well.

I have come to believe that the way Jesus answers that question "what will happen to us?" is to say: "In my physical absence, I am giving you one another to hold onto in this Christian journey. And I am giving you to one another in a way that supersedes the usual filial roles.

"Your family of discipleship will be your family of origin, your family of creation, and even greater. You will not only be present to one another in meeting those day-to-day needs, but you will understand and love each other through loving and understanding me. When you are passionate about the inseparable word-made-flesh, your brothers and sisters in Christ will understand. When your convictions of the heart don't work out, or when you feel that you are compromising too much or even when you feel you are compromising too little, the family I am giving you will understand."

We are the ones at that foot of the cross, the ones continually called to be there and in that shadow. We were included then, and we are included now, so that we might experience critical sorrow and critical love and critical discipleship.

I never figured out how to answer that little boy's question to me, at least in the temporal sense, except to be present with him in that question—to be present to pain and sadness and fear and, therefore, to enter into the shadow of the Crucifixion. I also know that as he longs to be with his mother again, he represents all of us at the foot of that Cross. For to live in that shadow is also, most importantly, to live in Resurrection Hope.

Woman, behold your Son. . . . Behold your Mother.

Journey Through Grief

by Suzanne Dillard Burke

Sometimes I go about pitying myself,
And all the time
I am being carried on great winds across
the sky -- Chippewa poem

STANDING ON A HILLTOP in Willamette National Cemetery I hear shots ring out, and then the distant hum of taps. Another veteran is being buried, as my husband, Dan, was one year ago. Low clouds add to the other-worldly feel of this sacred place. There is evidence that deer have been roaming between the graves, perhaps eating flowers at night. From this perspective, the world feels calm to me, in contrast to the turbulent, life-changing events of the past three years.

In the summer of 2007, Dan became seriously ill, was hospitalized and then, unable to return home, went to a nursing care center. For the next three years, I visited Dan daily, while working full-time, often commuting 100 miles a day. Finally in late-winter 2010 after a brave struggle, Dan died from an infection. My grief was not softened by his extended illness. I realized that I had been grieving throughout his illness for our former life together. But the reality of going on without him on the earth was far worse than I expected. My sadness was intensified by the loss of my long-term job and an injury that took away my mobility for six months.

As I stand at Dan's grave, my thoughts travel back to that time of caring for my husband and working full time. I was so discouraged and weary sometimes that I wasn't sure I could keep going. It was especially difficult knowing that there was only one outcome to the situation: Dan's death. But now, a year later, I can look back on that time with gratitude and some amazement. While the daily routine could be burdensome, there was so much going on beneath the surface, things that have changed me forever. I've learned more about faith, hope, and especially love than I ever imagined. I'd like to think that out of my struggles and sorrow that I will emerge a more sensitive and compassionate person. Time will tell.

This reflection is the story of my experiences with a dear loved one's illness and loss: the challenges we faced and the lessons I learned—and am still learning. I have not reached the end of my journey of grief. But I know I am already forever changed.

As I leave the cemetery, I watch large geese fly across the sky. I pray that someday I will again be able to soar.

Journey into Illness

In the summer of 2007, Dan and I had a good life. It moved with a calm and steady rhythm. Dan and I had been together for 30 years and were blessed to be best friends as well as husband and wife. While very different personalities, we would often finish each other's sentences. I was fulfilled in my career as a manager at a state agency dedicated to conservation and renewable energy. Dan worked hard at his own small business wholesaling tools and gloves. We were comfortable and happy in our split-level home in a suburb of Portland with a large, tree-filled yard and three cats. We appreciated having Dan's family 100 miles away in Eugene. After Dan miraculously recovered from a major stroke ten years before, we realized how fragile life is. We made several trips overseas and frequently visited family across the country. We had planned a trip to Spain and Morocco in the fall.

Then one moment changed everything. On the night of July 10, Dan came home from a doctor's appointment. The diagnosis was a large mass on his bladder. He also learned that his diabetes had worsened, and he would need to go on insulin. For a long time we sat on the couch, stunned. Finally, Dan said, "Let's go lie down," and we did, cold despite the hot summer night, silent and afraid.

In late July, I took a trip to visit former college roommates in South Carolina. I tried to relax, but was worried, preoccupied and unable to be reassured. I kept feeling that while Dan had always bounced back from danger, maybe this time we would not be so lucky. Being 3,000 miles apart, my one lifeline to Dan was my cell phone. Ironically, I fell into the ocean with the phone in my pocket, which ended our link for the rest of that trip. It felt like a bad omen.

Dan quickly was scheduled for exploratory surgery. The outcome of the biopsy was not good. The large mass was malignant and had gone into his bladder wall.

Dan decided on surgery to remove his entire bladder with the cancerous tumor. He made it through the nine-surgery successfully and talked with his son Erik and me in the Intensive Care Unit afterwards. But the next day delirium set in, and for the next ten days Dan had hallucinations and spoke in a wild, disconnected way. It was frightening for all of us. When he was finally back to normal, Dan was anxious to be released from the hospital. I was grateful for his improvement, but apprehensive about the care that I would need to give him, hoping I would be capable.

Dan was only home for six days. Those turned out to be his last six days in our home. One morning he woke up especially weak, light-headed and agitated. Late in the afternoon, I encouraged Dan to go lie down. Just before reaching our bed, he collapsed on the floor. At the time, getting him off the floor seemed the most important thing; if we could only do that, I told myself, everything would be okay. It was a tremendous effort, but finally, pale and sweaty, Dan was on the bed. Then I called the ambulance. The attendants said I shouldn't have tried to move him. As we drove back to the hospital we were also journeying deeper into a new territory, the world of grave illness.

The return trip to the hospital was the beginning of a medical roller coaster that would continue for the rest of Dan's life. Serious setbacks would be followed by promising recovery offset by more complications. Our hopes would soar only to crash again.

This time also marked a shift in our relationship. Dan was always more outgoing and talkative than I was. Known by his fierce intelligence and Irish gift of conversation, he relished being the more public person, taking on issues, finding solutions to problems, and being the protector. But now, clearly I needed to be his advocate. In the unknown and frightening world of hospitals, it was a big job. Throughout his illness, Dan remained himself at his core. But his ability to understand what was happening and to communicate was greatly diminished.

After Dan's second release from the hospital, he was not sent home but to a rehabilitation center in

King City. We entered in hopefully, but soon had our eyes opened to another strange new world. The facility was dreary and understaffed, with labyrinth hallways like a nightmare from which you could not wake up. Dan's spirits were good. He spoke Yiddish with the middle-aged woman doctor on duty. But he also refused to eat or drink much, a point of great contention for the family. Urging Dan to eat and drink made him defensive and angry. After six days he was sent by ambulance to Providence Hospital severely dehydrated, bleeding internally and with kidneys that were failing.

We spent almost a month at Providence. At one point, Dan asked if all the rooms in our house were connected to the hospital. The month in Providence was filled with hope and then fear and intense discussions with medical staff. An emotional young Irish doctor summed up this time when he said, "How much can one person take? We haven't given up yet, but at some point we may just want to make Dan comfortable. There have been an extraordinary number of setbacks!"

Deeper into Illness

Just before Thanksgiving, Dan was released to another nursing home. Life was more complicated. He now carried with him a feeding tube for nutrition, a bag to collect urine and failed kidneys that required dialysis.

While apprehensive about leaving the hospital, we were hopeful that Dan might get the care he needed to be able to come home. We visited on Thanksgiving Day and promised Dan we would bring white turkey meat and mashed potatoes the next day. It was heartbreaking to realize that Dan didn't truly understand why he couldn't come home with us.

The next day, I awoke to a message that Dan had gotten out of bed during the night and taken a bad fall injuring his back. He had been sent to the hospital and then returned to the nursing home. He was sedated but in great pain and could barely communicate. This setback was devastating. It compromised Dan's ability to participate in rehabilitation in the early, critical weeks. Shortly before Christmas, I learned that insurance would no longer cover Dan's care. The doctor and care team had determined that he could not benefit from any further rehabilitation. At the same time, Dan developed an infection, which caused him to be remote and unable to communicate. The end of the year was dark and frightening without much cause for hope.

"In our darkest hour it is often the smallest spark that brings with it the gift of light, be it ever so frail a flicker." -- Joyce Rupp

During my Christmas Eve visit, Dan had been mostly unaware of the holiday. Returning home, I sat in my driveway with a lump in my throat, not wanting to go into my dark, quiet house. Finding a message on my phone was a surprise, as I assumed most family members would be deep into their own celebrations. The words of the message, from a new friend who had just moved to Oregon, wished me comfort and blessings. That message was a ray of light in that bleak day.

Another ray of light came from periodic improvements in Dan's condition. On New Year's Eve, based on conversations with the doctor, Dan's sister Candy and I were certain we would lose him soon. So, my heart leapt with joy when I came in later that week to find Dan was up in the hallway, joking with staff and exercising.

Early in our stay, I realized the nursing staff was providing constant flickers of light. Vivian, the Resident Care Manager on the first floor, found a private room for Dan on the second floor. We did not hesitate to take it, as it was light-filled with a view of trees and neighborhood houses. It was touching to realize that Vivian did not want to see us go as she had bonded with us and considered us "hers." But she wanted us to be comfortable. A sad underlying message of the move was that the second floor was for permanent residents; those who had little or no hope of ever going home.

New Challenges

Letting go of the hope of recovery was perhaps the biggest challenge. Initially, Dan was still participating in physical therapy, walking down the hallway, using the bathroom on his own. But with time all of his capabilities gradually declined. The most ordinary things became difficult. One day, Dan was in bed sitting rather crookedly when he asked me to help him take off his green chamois shirt. He couldn't lift himself far enough and the shirt was stuck behind his back and shoulders. Dan kept extending his arms and insisting we could "solve this problem."

Frustrated to tears, I told him that we were just going to have to chill out until we could get some help. I pushed the call light.

To my surprise, Dan said "Okay, let's sing a song then!"

I asked "What do you want to sing?" and he proceeded to sing "When Irish Eyes Are Smiling." While he had trouble remembering things like where he had lived and worked, he sang the lyrics from start to finish. I asked him what made him think of that song. He smiled and replied "Oh, your Irish eyes!"

That spring when I completed our taxes and asked Dan to sign them, the moment he picked up a pen we realized he was no longer able to sign his name. It was an unexpected shock and sadness for both of us.

Accustomed to an independent life, adjusting to life in a nursing home was not easy. While privacy was respected ("knock first"), it was a concept more than a reality. Staff had constant access to the room for a myriad of services. Overall, we fell into the rhythm of the facility, establishing routines and attending events such as music classes, Bingo, and ice cream socials. We became close to the many caring people who watched over Dan daily.

Still, especially on his energetic days, Dan was restless. One afternoon I asked:

"Do you want to come home?"

"Of course I do. I don't want to be in this wilderness."

"Wilderness?"

"Well it is."

"Why?"

"It just is."

"Are people kind to you?"

"Oh yes, very kind. I have no comments."

"No comments?"

"No complaints. No complaints at all."

Meanwhile, on Good Friday I felt I was in my own wilderness praying for hope and strength. The biggest challenge was the fragility of Dan's health. I started unplugging the phone at night, rather than lying awake waiting for it to ring. In the morning, I would re-connect the phone, full of dread until I knew there was no call with bad news waiting.

On Holy Saturday that year, thick white snowflakes fell into the white blossoms of the crabapple tree in my front yard. On Easter morning

64

the blossoms had survived the last show of winter. It seemed a hopeful omen.

Perhaps the biggest challenge was adjusting to our new life with each other. No longer able to get out and do even the most ordinary of things, Dan was transported everywhere by stretcher. Accompanying him to medical appointments became the closest thing we had to a date.

Time flowed on with the seasons in the nursing home. Medical issues caused many trips to the hospital. A brain scan showed what we suspected: Dan had considerable damage from one large stroke and a number of small ones or possibly from diabetes or the delirium that followed his surgery. Still, he managed to be remarkably oriented and loving.

We adapted to the life that we still had and, if Dan had not gotten worse, could have continued with that life for much longer. But, his condition was steadily worsening. By the fall of 2009, his options were running out. Despite additional surgeries and rigorous treatments with antibiotics for infections, in early March 2010, Dan was put on hospice care. After such a long struggle to keep him alive, we had to help him die peacefully. It was necessary, inevitable but wrenching.

On March 11, 2010 Dan passed away early in the morning with his son Erik sleeping in the room.

Lessons Learned

The entire experience of caring for Dan through his illness and death will be with me for the rest of my life. These lessons are simple but felt deeply in my heart.

The Comfort of Faith: Living with death so near, it was a comfort to be part of a faith community with a belief in the promise of eternal life. It did not take away the deep sadness I felt about losing Dan, but it did soften the fear. During Dan's illness, I was touched by the prayers that were constantly with us: from members of my Jesuit Catholic parish, my women's spirituality group, family and friends.

"I know well the plans I have in mind for you, says the Lord. Plans for your welfare, not for woe! Plans to give you a future full of hope." -- *Jeremiah 29:11*

One parishioner, Mary, a 75-year old Irish woman with a lilting voice, regularly came to see Dan. How she managed to appear when we most needed her I'll never know—it could only be God's grace. Once Dan's youngest brother had just died, and we were holding each other and crying when Mary walked in the door. Another time we were tensely awaiting a ride to the hospital, and there was Mary. She also prayed alone with Dan, and he seemed to enjoy it.

Half Irish and half Polish, Dan grew up in an ethnic neighborhood in Lawrence, Massachusetts, a mill town about an hour north of Boston. He also had an affinity for Jewish culture, honed by work when he was young in kosher hotels in the Catskills. Dan has been described spiritually as an ethnic Catholic with a Yiddish soul. By education, he believed deeply in science and rationality. And yet, preparing for an operation, Dan solemnly asked, "Who is going to pray for me? I want Yiddish prayers and Christian prayers."

The Persistence of Hope: Hope is what enabled me to see beyond the current moment, however bleak, and know that things would be okay somehow. Often an unexpected kind word, a phone call, or good deed would buoy me up. One day while waiting for transport to the hospital, frustrated that I had forgotten my lunch, I rushed to use the vending machines in the employee lunch room. A maintenance man, whom I barely knew, interrupted his own lunch and went to the refrigerator insisting with a huge smile that I take some of his homemade soup. It fed my soul as well as my body.

The Power of Love: Perhaps the most enduring lesson I learned was about love. Love endures; love evolves and continues into eternity.

Frequently I was touched by the love of others, helping me in a difficult situation even if they were afraid. Illness can hit too close to home. Some family members were a lifeline, always reaching out. Others were less steady, but gave from their hearts. Then there are the aides and nurses who care for the frail and ill with great tenderness and often little financial reward. I will never forget how they cared for Dan until the end.

One of the biggest surprises was that the love my husband and I had for each other continued to evolve and grow. One day early in his stay at the nursing home, Dan held his arm up high.

I asked, "What are you doing, Dan?"

"I'm just trying to connect with you," he said.

We held hands tightly.

Despite ever-increasing illness, our connection was always strong. Dan would introduce me to staff with pride. When a music therapist asked, "Dan, is it good to see your wife?" he replied, "Oh yes. Wonderful! Jolly!"

One Saturday morning when Dan was still in bed, I was sitting at his bedside feeling a little sorry for myself when Nadine, a young Jamaican aide, looked at me and said in her musical voice "I hope I can find someone who loves me as much as he loves you. Not everybody loves their wife like that."

I was taken aback and could only respond, "I'm lucky."

"You are lucky," she said.

We kept in touch with other family members mostly by phone. Concerned about how easily Dan tired, I asked if he enjoyed the phone calls. He replied, "Oh yes, there is so much love in them."

As Dan became more ill, he slept more. Often when I arrived at his room, I would awaken him. As his eyes opened, he would get a beautiful smile on his face. It felt like pure love, not diluted with any expectations. To see that smile, and respond to it, is the closest I will get in this world to understanding God's unconditional love.

In Dan's final hospitalization, he still showed joy when I visited. One day as I walked in the room, Dan yelled as if from a great distance, "Suzanne, I'm over here! Over here!"

The nurse Michael said, "That is the first time I've seen him smile. That's wonderful!" At moments like that I could imagine God welcoming each of us home with that kind of joy.

Throughout Dan's illness I came to feel gratitude for each day, each moment that we still had together. I treasure his words to me when I was sad: "Our love will be there forever and ever. Nothing can change that."

Journey into the Future

"As in the world around us, so too in human life, darkness is followed by light and sorrow by consolation." – Gates of Prayer, Rabbi Chaim Stern, editor.

Now I look to a future that I need to create myself. I have moved through sorrow and received much consolation. It would not be realistic to say that I have left sorrow behind. My heart is not completely mended and perhaps never will be.

I do believe that the struggles of the past few years—shared by family and friends—have given me a foundation to move ahead. Losing a beloved spouse is not an unusual experience, but may be one of the most painful ones that many of us have to face. Since the worst happened and I came through, I have a greater faith that I can deal with other difficult situations. I now have a greater belief in the essential goodness of people and have learned better how to ask for help.

The sadness in my spirit lifts occasionally with special waves of energy and interest in creating a new, meaningful life. It won't be easy or happen overnight. But I will carry all the experiences of love and loss and sorrow with me into all that lies ahead.

Blessed with Blindness

by Karen Gatens

A SEARCH IMPLIES that you don't know where something is, and if you don't know where something is, you don't know what or how long it will take to get it. The search requires blindness. In art school I took a course in fiber arts. Weaving seemed rather easy to me, but it took 35 hours to create a piece 10 inches x 13 inches. If I had known how long it would take to complete the project, I would have stopped myself from ever starting. It was in that class that I realized the immense value of ignorance.

When I was asked to write a bit about what I had learned in life, I jumped on my computer and responded affirmatively without thinking. I cried. I felt blessed. I felt this was a sign that I could and should "come out" about my ever-evolving, culturally diverse spiritual path. I scurried to my journal and began a retrospect of all the crevices and turns of a search for that illuminating presence I call "God." But after several weeks of writing, the lines on my forehead were more numerous than the lines of this chapter. From enthusiasm to share a myriad of mysteries, mystics and miracles, I went to questioning what the heck was the point of me saying a darn thing. What did I know anyway? The flow started to dribble as the judgments came. I started and stopped, started and stopped and soon the joy of revealing my experiences was replaced by mental flagellation.

Wandering, wavering and waffling are my personal prerequisites to completing a creative task—wandering through the desert in search of water and, upon finding the water hole, doubting that it's safe to drink. The Old Testament says it took the Jews 40 years to pass through the Sinai desert. An ambitious team of biblical scholars decided to take the walk themselves and found that it took 11 days. The Jews did a lot of starting and stopping, too. But I forget that.

How do you search with ignorance as a guide? When you don't know where you belong or where you're going, you discover faith. In fact, all people have faith. We don't really know much of anything and certainly not what God is or a planet or water. We experience an event or an element or a being and call it by a name to identify a common understanding in the same way that I am identified as "Karen." I have a particular form with certain characteristics. Mostly we believe what we think is, in fact, true. We use our logic to reason it. We add information to this kernel. Build it into theories and then fight for it. What we believe to be true keeps us intact. It's like gravity. When we don't know, we believe. We fill in the blanks. Some believe in love or justice or reason or religion or God or effort or patience or bliss or discipline. I believe in longing. It's this missing part that holds the secret to beliefs and purpose.

When I was 17, I was kicked out of my religion class and called a heretic. After my senior year in high school, I announced to a priest that I was going away to college to lose my faith and if I ever found it again, it would be my own. I didn't know I would lose myself and all that I had identified as real in search of something to satisfy the restless longing for a raison d'etre. I crept out of my traditional Catholic upbringing "with fear and trembling" and intentionally skipped my first Mass at age 18. I didn't die.

Depression hit me as soon as I left home and moved to Seattle where I attended the University of Washington. I found that God—Jesus to be exact—wasn't helping me out of it either. I decided I needed true love in the shape of a cute boy, and then I would live happily now and in the ever after. Instead in my first term, I put on 30 pounds; no boy was eyeing me at this new weight. I started to smoke. Then I started to smoke other things. So I gave up the weight problem in exchange for a smoking problem that took many more years to correct. I hid my shame, meshed it with anger at God and blamed my dear father for my dark mood and weight gain. My thoughts centered around me and my growing misery, though I pretended all was well. I felt the dense weight of an internal elephant that couldn't find an opening to leave. I prayed God would take pity on me, lift my depressed state, give me purpose, give me my mate and help me lose weight. Wasn't He sovereign? Wouldn't He leave his flock to help one sheep? I dropped out of college.

God did hear me at 20, and I found myself in the born-again movement of the 70's. While the woman's movement was shouting for liberation and civil rights were pointing the way to equality, the Holy Spirit was flooding the streets of Berkeley. California turned from the protests of the Vietnam War to a downpouring of the charismatic. What was once a corner store handing out anti-war literature was now a Baha'i dry cleaner or a Buddhist cafe or a Hindu grocery store. I ended up living in a Born-again Christian commune.

According to my Protestant elders, I was "saved by grace through faith." All I had to do was believe in Jesus. What a dose of freedom! No mortal sin would take me to hell. In a tiny town in Northern California, I encountered the supernatural world of demons, faith healers, the language of tongues and bible studies. Moments of honest joy bated my spiritual appetite followed by surprised frustration as my beloved non-Christian books were burned. I soon left the commune, but still held to the new-found idea that I was saved as long as I believed in Jesus as the only Son of God. In the years that followed, I became aware that belief was not the same as faith and that miracles—honest-to-goodness, make-your-mouth-drop-open miracles—do not make a person virtuous.

Confused by the contradiction of feeling free to "just believe" and the simultaneous restriction of believing in any other teachings, I returned to school in Seattle. Then one morning, out of the blue, I woke up with an urge to learn Hebrew. It came like a shooting star, quickly and brilliantly. A week later I met a Brooklyn-born, yeshiva-educated Jew. He was ridding himself of his traditional upbringing as I was trying to rewrap myself in a new and improved version of Christianity—not quite born-again, but no longer on my way to purgatory or worse. Life was good; God had heard me. But all the born-again Christians thought differently. Instead, they predicted tragedy for the believer who perched with a non-believer; the branch would break. I left these nay-sayers behind, worried that they were right, and we got married.

It was through my then-husband that I met a man who would act as my spiritual sage and surrogate father for the next 26 years—until he died. John C. Little was born on the charcoal-poor side of the tracks in East St. Louis. He had grown up a preacher's son, but his father died when he was about 10 years old. Punished often by teachers for laziness due to his undiagnosed dyslexia, he dropped out of school about age 12. By the time he died, John Little had been appointed to the President's Council for Humanity, was an honorary professor at Western Washington State, had developed ideas that became state law regarding the treatment of delinquents, had developed inner city 4-H outdoor youth programs and had a park named after him in Seattle. Beyond that, he and his wife raised 14 foster children and seven of his own. His wisdom and comfort make me weep to this day.

John had studied the teachings of Yogananda, a missionary from India who largely established yoga in the U.S. Though he returned to his Baptist roots, he did so with enlightened insight into Christ's message of redemption and assured me that God could handle my questioning explorations and that there was only one God who made all, regardless of their particular brand of religion or non-religion. It was up to me to decide. He listened and counseled me during one of the most difficult periods of my life. Within a three-month period, I was ravaged by an unfaithful husband and subsequent divorce, an arson fire that destroyed our business, major surgery, a car theft and job loss that catapulted me into deep depression and rejection of the Christian God that was supposed to give me my "heart's desires."

At the depth of my depression he told me I was "just arrogant." Hurt and stunned, I couldn't understand how this depression could be considered a symptom of pride. "If you could do better, you would," he softly said. I was weakened by grief, fear and loneliness, so that my heart could be stretched open; later to be filled with greater compassion and patience for in "our weakness we are made strong." Years later

I realized that God was not my personal genie and that our false truisms are often peeled away like the shocking sting of a bandage.

The God that I had believed in did not comfort me, so I sought answers elsewhere. I turned to art, Jungian psychology and my dreams. With the study of my dreams came much self-analysis and intrigue but little comfort. Then on a knoll in a wooded area of inner Seattle, a mini-miracle occurred. A scream deep in my psyche reached the surface and I bellowed, "God, give me freedom!"

It came audibly: "Even atheists can get to God."

I heard myself think, *What is that supposed to mean!? What does my freedom have to do with atheists going to heaven?! God must have tuned into the wrong channel!*" This was not the expected answer, and it puzzled me for months, but I noticed that the guilt grip of my Christian teachings had loosened. Without knowing, I had been given permission to seek God outside of a Christian context. I would learn to "know them by their fruits" because "God is spirit, and those who worship Him must worship in spirit and truth."

From this viewpoint, I attended a Buddhist lecture and had my first lesson in meditation. The teacher was so joyful.

"I can't discipline myself to practice meditation," I told him.

"You have to discipline yourself. Freedom only comes through discipline," he said gleefully.

It bored me, made me feel incompetent, rather hopeless; I didn't get it. I was 31. But I heard something that I had never heard before—a value paramount in any spiritual understanding of the self. The monk explained that we are not our emotions, we must let them pass through us. We must not say, "I am sad," we must not identify with the sadness as being ourselves. This is what "letting go" means. But I wasn't letting go yet, I was still grieving the loss of my marriage and, more importantly, the loss of what I believed to be true.

My wayward path led me to a devotee of Paramahansa Yoganada. "I was washing dishes one day," she said, "and I realized that I was hurrying to get the dishes done, so I could hurry to the next unpleasant task to get that done, so I could get to the next one and the next one until I could get all my unpleasant tasks completed, so I could get to the ones that were pleasurable. I decided I wanted to be happy regardless of the task at hand."

"*Wow*," I thought, "*that's pretty insightful. But is it possible?*"

Eventually, I made a prolonged visit to the self-realization community of Ananda in the hills of California to find out. Many seemed to have found that state of unpretentious contentment, and I wanted it, too.

Meditation came easier there and for about two minutes, I tasted ecstatic bliss. You'd think that one would be appreciative after such a blessed gift, but I was upset. "How could You let me taste Your life and then take it away?!" One can never depend upon a repeat experience from God nor seek one. And an experience is never an indicator of one's holiness but only an entrance as to what is available to us as part of the human species.

Meditation stops things. Finally I stopped asking for my purpose or to find the love of my life or passion or even peace. When we stop, we don't move. When we don't move, we aren't restless. When we aren't restless, we are at peace.

I returned to my hectic life in Seattle and watched my meditation practice dwindle. But I now acknowledged the divinity of the miracles and teachings of Hindu mystics. I had dipped my mind into the possibility of the manifestation of God in a man other than Jesus and of reincarnation. I wasn't sure if I believed these two heretical ideas, but they made sense.

Our universe operates cyclically. Consider the cycle of planets, the seasons of the year, menstruation, the water cycle, the nitrogen cycle, sleep cycles, oxygen-carbon dioxide cycles, salmon spawning and the migration of birds and animals. Since science tells us energy is always conserved, we must live in some state, somehow, somewhere. Even Catholicism teaches that there is a holding ground after life, i.e. purgatory, where we work out our imperfections until we enter heaven. Why not just cycle around earth again? As Christ said, "And if you are willing to accept it, John himself is Elijah who was to come. He who has ears to hear, let him hear." Matt.11:14-15

Life moved forward and backward and after four-and-a-half years of 60-hour workweeks, I needed a break. I discussed the possibility of an extended absence with my employer, found someone to take my place as an interim art department manager, bought a round-trip ticket and prepared for a two-month visit to the Indian ashram of the great guru, Sai Baba. I was ill but functional, or so I tried to be. At this time, my breathing was labored and short, shadows rimmed my eyes, my ears ached as did my stomach, and I wore coats in the office to keep from freezing—but my will would carry me to India. I thought if I could just find a guru, I would be well—that it was a test of my faith and determination. All my ducks were lined up. It was ten days before I would fly out of Seattle and back to my mother's home for Christmas. I would then return to Seattle and fly to India!

Arriving at the Public Health Office to receive my final immunization shot, the nurse looked at me and said "I won't give you this shot; you have to go to the emergency ward."

What? Wait a minute. Whose side are you on, God? I'm going to be healed by a holy man and feel Your life pour through me… Right? But I went to the emergency room.

I was to be hospitalized, but instead bartered my hospital stay for a visit to a specialist the next day. The doctor listened with interest as I relayed my plans to go to India.

When I finished, he calmly said, "You can go to India;" as I began to light up, he completed, "and you'll die."

Even then I kept thinking this was a test, until a wise woman said, "Honor the obvious." My choice was die or go back to Reno, where my mother would care for me.

About three weeks after I got to Reno, a dear friend contacted me with information about a job being advertised in the Seattle Times that sounded like mine. It was mine! *"What?!"* burst through my brain. Suddenly there was no reason to return to Seattle. I was cut off from my job, my health, my identity, my friends, my life of the last 15 years and left in the dust of Reno, a place I had fled after high school. No one knew I had been the art department manager for a prestigious winery in the Northwest. There were no sales people clambering to meet me; no designers, illustrators or photographers making requests to review their portfolios. This was not my plan for healing or love or happiness at age 37.

"Maybe your illness is your guru?" a friend suggested.

No! God made another mistake.

Doctors kept giving me medications that did nothing but irritate my stomach. My immune system had cracked. I had abused my body with cigarettes, caffeine, drugs of the 70's, overeating, junk food, lack of exercise, too much work and lack of sleep. I had done this to myself, and the responsibility was mine to fix. I began to search for a way to heal. Reading books and seeking alternative options, I put myself on a rigid diet eliminating all dairy, all caffeine, all alcohol, all fermented foods and beverages, all yeast, all processed foods, all night shade plants, all legumes, all sugar including fruit. I was left with whole grains, greens, lemons, almonds and olive oil. For eight months, I did not veer from this limited diet. I discovered that what I put into my body to help cure it was not important, if I did not remove what harmed it. We are self-regulating beings.

Elimination is at the heart of meditation, be it Centering Prayer or Vipassana or Hong Sau or Vedic. It is the essence of detachment. De-clutter and you gain space—the only unchanging constant. Space holds everything and allows everything to freely move. In order to know the space, we let go of the thoughts, the feelings, the sensations of the physical body.

God did not intervene to cure me instantaneously, nor would Sai Baba. It was hard work. And had I known how long it would take or that I would need to eliminate not only food, but social patterns, attachment to my work, my identity and many friends, like with the weaving project in art school, I wouldn't have started.

This is where God is—in the space that holds our moving parts—be they rough or soiled or broken or incurable, in between our thoughts, in the missing parts of our lives, in the undercurrent. We often don't see the underlying blessings given to us in our life, because they don't always come manifest as joy or love or enthusiasm. More often they come disguised as dissatisfaction, confusion, doubt, frustration, irritation, and even anger to push us into action. Like the oyster that coats a grain of sand with the fluids of its own body, we create our pearls from the distress of our lives.

I have struggled to find my purpose, to find love, to find passion, to find that "peace that surpasses all things," that inspiration or person or belief that holds me so tightly with such love, security and tenderness that I find no reason to leave. I had expected that God would fulfill "the desires of my heart" if I kept begging, pleading, pouting, but instead I was given two failed marriages, illness, a fire, depression and a myriad of bumps. However, in between, in the gaps, I was given the ability to let go, to laugh at myself, to take responsibility, to forgive, to parent a beautiful daughter, to do good, to be open to other cultures and beliefs, to find strength when I had none, to learn patience, to gain gratitude, to halt judgment and to remember that I am first a soul—with a body, mind and emotions.

Eight months after arriving back in my hometown of Reno, my father died. I would never have returned to Reno were it not for ill health; never would have been able to spend extended time with him, meet the father of my daughter nor get well. But if I were God, I would have done it differently. "For My thoughts are not your thoughts, nor are your ways My ways,' declares the LORD." Isaiah 55:8

What Death Can Teach Us About Life

by Sherold Barr

*Grandfather, Great Spirit, You have set the
power of the four quarters of the earth to cross
each other. You have made me cross the good
road, and the road of difficulties,
and where they cross, the place is holy.
Day in and day out, forevermore,
you are the life of things.
– Black Elk, Oglala Sioux*

SIX YEARS AGO my brother Byron disappeared. He went from being my baby brother to a missing person to a homicide victim. His body was missing for three years before it was found on a remote farm near Knoxville, Tennessee, and in 2008, he became a cold case statistic.

This family tragedy is one of approximately 6,800 cold cases left unsolved each year. These horror stories have no ending and no closure for many families. We know this firsthand.

Byron was last seen on May 3, 2005. My family's calls to him went unanswered for more then a week, and when they were answered, his roommate told us

Byron had just stepped out. And that he was fine. Of course, we found later that this was a lie.

My husband and I were set to fly to Barcelona, Spain, on May 18. Just before I left the country, I made a last, quick call to my mother to say goodbye. She was very upset, having returned from Byron's apartment, which was wrecked as if a fight had taken place. Byron was gone.

I knew in that moment something tragic had happened to my brother. I just somehow knew it. Leaving the country that day, my heart heavy, I began a five-year voyage into the dark night of my soul.

I walked around Barcelona in a fog, glued to my Blackberry, hoping for news. When it came, it hit me like soul shrapnel. Byron's car had been found in another state with a substantial amount of blood in the trunk. His case went from a missing person to a homicide.

Mom went in for a DNA blood test. Can you imagine waiting for the results of a DNA test to determine if your child was murdered? As a mother myself, I could hardly imagine the horror. The stranger who killed her son was also guilty of ripping out a piece of her heart that would never be replaced. She said to me later, "I can't believe I'll never see Byron on this earth again."

The night Byron's car was found I lay in bed staring at the ceiling while horrendous scenarios played out in my mind. I envisioned Byron's body in a fetal position in the trunk. He had been beaten. I felt his panic as he lay injured and locked in the dark trunk driving to the unimaginable . . . I could not have imagined the truth: he was shot in the head and thrown out in a field behind a shack exactly like the one on the cover of the bestseller, *The Shack*.

Our lives changed in an instant to a living CSI television show. We were traumatized and in deep shock.

Martha Beck calls this a catalytic event. A shock, a death, divorce, a birth or marriage, these all are major turning points in our lives, whether negative or positive. But when a death is sudden, unexpected, or in this case, violent, the most traumatic grief occurs. Deaths that are mutilating or destructive, especially when caused by the actions of another person, lead to a more complicated mourning process for families. This is exacerbated in instances where there is no body and no closure.

My family and I entered the liminal period—a time in which we couldn't go back, yet we couldn't go forward. Friends do not know what to say, so for those who have suffered a violent crime, it's a lonely time, accompanied by guilt and shame. The liminal period is extremely important for grief work. It's a transitional time and when we eventually pass through it, it brings renewed life.

My mother has suffered the most challenges of Byron's death. "The mother of a murdered child also suffers this archetypal experience of the earth being pulled from under herself—fundamentally sullied by intimate association with the archetypal evil deed," notes Charlotte Mathes in *A Sword Shall Pierce Your Heart*. When you lose your parents, you lose your history. When you lose your child, you lose your future.

The search for meaning after a violent crime can challenge survivors' religious or spiritual beliefs. Death is the numinous—it is filled with deep associations with God and the mysterious unknowing. Thankfully my mother has her faith, and this has helped carry her through. I discovered a deeper connection to God, my family and myself and have taken a deep dive into my own conscious and unconscious life.

As for me, I am grateful for my wonderful Jungian analyst with whom I have worked these last six years to help me with the grief process, and to make sense of this horrific tragedy. I record and we interpret my dreams to reveal what my unconscious is showing me.

My life and my career changed utterly the day Byron disappeared. Instead of pursuing a master's degree that fall, I slowly downsized my PR business to work on projects that I alone could manage. It was all I could do to cope. In fact, coping mechanisms flew out the window—they do at times like these.

It would be two years before I attended a workshop to search for a whisper of inspiration. Then I heard about Martha Beck and her life coach training. In 2007 and 2008, I went through two of her trainings and became a master life coach. It was with Martha that I learned about "The Work" of Byron Katie.

In a powerful workshop with Katie, I was finally able to let go of the mind movies I was playing about Byron's murder. I learned that each time I created scary pictures in my mind of how I imagined he was killed, I was murdering him over and over again. So I was re-traumatizing myself over and over again. I fantasized, longing for Byron's killer to be found, put in prison, to suffer for this crime. But experiencing "The Work" of Byron Katie, I realized I was the one in prison as long as I continued to communicate with the investigator to keep Bryon's case alive.

In our technologically advanced society, we live in our minds and believe our thoughts. Our bodies don't know if we are experiencing trauma for the first time or the 100th time. So each time the mind pulls up the movie of the trauma, the body goes into flight and fight mode once again.

It took me five long years to return to what felt like my normal self and to move out of deep grief. I dove into personal growth as a way to make some sort of sense of this tragedy. I slowly came to the decision that I would work with other women to help them live their best life while doing the same for myself. So, through this hard process of healing, I discovered and embraced a new career.

What I have learned is that out of darkness, there really is light. Bad things in life can lead to good things. I would not be a life or business coach if my brother had not died. I would have continued in the corporate world and not gained my current depth of personal and spiritual growth.

Has a difficult and trying time brought forth something positive in your life? Or are you still searching for answers?

If you follow the steps outlined below, I believe you will someday reach closure and healing as I have.

How to Transform Traumatic Grief Into A Renewed Life

Be kind to yourself. Be sure to recognize that the experience of a sudden or violent traumatic event in your life may have left you with posttraumatic stress syndrome in addition to grief. You may find yourself trapped in your thoughts, ruminating over and over in your mind, and your sense of safety could be disrupted.

You **can** come through this dark time. You may even discover a deeper, more meaningful life. As I have done.

Here are ten tips that may help you. These I have gained from my own experience, and from the work of respected grief and trauma specialists:

1. **Maintain as normal routine as possible.** A traumatic death creates the sense of loss of control. Try to re-establish normal routines so you feel that you have more control of your life.

2. **Put structure in your day.** Even if you don't feel like working out or exercising, try to get back to your regular schedule as much as possible. When my friend and employee, Betsy, lost her 51-year-old husband to sudden cardiac arrest, I was at a loss how to help her. Since exercise is a great stress-reducer, I decided to give her a year's membership to an athletic club. Betsy told me years later that it saved her—gave her structure though a very difficult time.

3. **Feel the feelings.** Emotions are the language of our body. I call them our emotional GPS system. So, try to welcome *all* your emotions in a compassionate way. Understand that they are natural after what you have gone through. Emotions help us connect to our body, and although sometimes you will want to stop feeling the feelings you are experiencing, just know that if push them away, they'll persist and may even come up in inappropriate ways. You may begin to act them out. So give them your attention and the process time they need.

4. **Practice some form of mindfulness or meditation.** I started listening to a Yoga Nidra CD every night. Yoga Nidra is a deep form of meditation that has been found in scientific studies to help PTSD and ADHD. It releases negative emotions and thought patterns, calms the nervous system, and helps

you develop a deeper capacity to meet any and all circumstances you may encounter in life. For more information, visit http://irest.us.

5. **Practice Yoga**. Practicing yoga can help you connect back to your body. There are many varieties of yoga, which combine exercise with mindfulness to provide relaxation and a sense of peace. I practice Anusara and Hatha Yoga, which has been one of the most beneficial things I've done, in addition to listening to Yoga Nidra CDs. I've started a practice I expect to continue throughout my life.

6. **Create a living story of your loved one**. Instead of the traumatic death story, think of the positive and deeply meaningful experiences you've had with the person you've lost. This is not to idealize them. In fact, it is important to recognize what you didn't care for about this person—what irritated you. This keeps reality in place. Create a new story to replace whatever traumatic details are involved in the way this person may have died. Telling a beautiful story, while recognizing that they, too, were human is another way to heal. Storytelling can bring order and meaning. Nothing can take away the experiences you had with this person in your life. Highlight what you want to remember.

7. **Write a letter to your loved one who died.** Express what you were not able to say to them and all they meant to you. Through your letter, feel a bond with the friend or family member you lost. Having this imaginary conversation with your loved one is very healing and begins to bring closure.

8. **Stop playing traumatic mind movies.** Our deeper mind can't know if you are reliving the trauma for the first time or the 100th time. If you can retell the story and stay present at the same time, without having all the negative feelings, then you will begin to experience some peace. You may even find you can talk about it without falling apart. Learn to tell the details of what happened in a different way so you have a different relationship with them. You will begin to disconnect from the trauma of the story.

9. **Stop feeling guilty (if you are).** I like to ask my clients, "What are you making this mean?" Find out what the fear or belief is underneath the guilt or shame. If you believe it's your fault or you are feeling guilt then you must disconnect from the story. Can you discover a new mission or purpose out of this experience?

10. **Get involved in community.** Trauma is powerfully transformed by connecting with others, and by giving and receiving compassion. We tend to withdraw into ourselves, like sick animals, during times of grief. But needing and being needed is very comforting, and the bond can soothe. So get connected in a group—happiness lies in serving others outside yourself. You will be served by that serving of others! With a group focus on "How can we grow from this experience?" you may speed your path to healing.

Good luck and God-speed.

"No one ever really dies as long as they took the time to leave us with fond memories." – Chris Sorensen

Even Good Girls Get The Blues

by Lola Scobey

You cannot look to the world itself as the source of your life. The world and its strategies may help you to survive for a long time, but they cannot help you live because the world is not the source even of its own life, let alone yours. – Henri J. M. Nouwen

ONE RAINY MORNING, despite a long and meaningful 25-year journey of faith, I woke up and simply wondered if I could go on.

Feelings of despair and failure rose up like the recent tsunamis and rolled over me in heavy strangling waves. The undertow pulled me emotionally back and down, dragging me far out from any visible shore and away from important things.

I knew this wasn't just another trough on the rollercoaster that has characterized my spiritual journey—undulating ups and downs of doubt, discouragement, and fear interwoven with sturdier streams of faith, hope, and courage. This felt oddly fatal; scary, like an ending.

For three years I'd been in transition on so many levels of life, I'd lost count. An initially optimistic move two years ago from Colorado to Oregon had definitely asserted a mind of its own—refusing to go the way I'd planned; continually upending my assumptions about how things ought to work out.

Curled in bed in a fetal ball, I feared that pressure from 36 months of bombardment by constant change, coming fast on the heels of decades of dysfunctional chaos, had caused some layer inside me to finally crack. I lay there, unsure. Was this an exceptionally rough step on my spiritual journey? Or was this the collapse of my journey in confusion and failure?

It sure didn't feel like the positive evolution in myself I had hoped years of knowing God would bring. Transformation? The still center? Peace? No. I was feeling huge fissures in my image of who I was and who God is. It wasn't that what I saw was unnerving. It was that I was having trouble seeing anything recognizable at all.

And that was devastating. Because since 1985, I'd given my life to my journey with God.

Admittedly, just based on the facts of daily life, this particular morning was not one of my best. I'd recently sold the unique house on a waterfall up in the mountains of Colorado that my former husband and I designed, built, and owned together. I was so relieved to finally sell it. But about a week after the closing it hit me that, with the sale, my last tenuous tie to my old life had been cut. Amputated from my life. Severed. Like the term they use for baseball players, I was now a free agent. Sounds blissful after all the struggle to get there. But this was more like free floating. Untethered. On my own with nothing but this new amorphous life.

Sure, there were days I felt ready to conquer the world and launch a triumphant existence in my new hometown of Portland, Oregon. One that would prove I had made the right decision, despite giving up an all-consuming 30-year relationship that included 22 years of marriage, my stepchildren, and my recently built Colorado mountain home. One that proved I was capable of dancing right on up the ladder of success, despite leaving my career of the last two decades. One that proved I was right to move to a city where I only knew one person, and had no established clients for freelance work, no job to make ends meet, no church, no clubs, no structure of any kind waiting for me there. One that proved I had been right to believe God was guiding me.

On this morning I didn't feel capable of proving any of that. I was in a pit. A clammy, empty, echoing pit. Deserted. At the critical juncture of the biggest transition of my life, God seemed to have disengaged; gone elsewhere.

The 2000-mile drive from Colorado to Oregon marked the wrenching end of a long held dream. Although "dream" is too thin a word. The steady drive west signaled an unexpected plot twist in what I had believed to be an unchanging promise, a calling: my story with God.

This story began at a point that some consider nearing middle age. At that time, virtually every dimension of my life not grounded in core family relationships started over. All at once, in my late 30's, I (1) gave up a prominent career in the glitzy and glamorous music industry; (2) had 15 years of contented atheism flipped on its ear; (3) got married after 15 years of being single; (4) became a stepmother after a lifetime of choosing to have no children; and (5) launched a totally-against-the-odds pioneering business in the undeveloped field of music therapy with barely any financial resources. In one fell swoop.

Normally, this lunatic list would by itself declare me certifiably insane and explain any- and everything unexplainable or seemingly disastrous that has happened since. Except for one factor. What made this lunacy seem possible—even desirable to me—was an experience of encountering Jesus about six months prior.

Six months before, I was in the hit music business. I was an atheist. I was not seeking God. I was 39 and had not been inside a church since my early 20's. Religion seemed clearly irrational, and, far worse, utterly boring.

Then one night, in my historic little two-story Alabama house, I was propped up on pillows in bed reading. Around midnight, Jesus arrived. In maybe 3 minutes, my life flipped over on edge.

The voice. The voice was there, in my bedroom. Through the years, wandering outside in the woods, sitting under trees looking for fairies, searching in the pages of endless books, in church, in Christian high school, in Christian college, out of Christian college, in a teen marriage, out of teen marriage, into the university, into atheism, into philosophy graduate school, into the music business. All my life I had been hearing . . . something. At that moment, in my bedroom, somehow, I knew what it was. Or rather, Who it was. Calling. To me.

The next morning I got up and began leaving my job in the music business. It was no longer meaningful.

That personal encounter made all the resulting simultaneous changes seem not merely possible—but compelling. The whole upheaval felt like both a calling and a long-term promise. I was being unexpectedly delivered into a new life. Like an Israelite being led out of Egypt to serve God. Just like in the Bible.

True, as months passed this new life did indeed seem to involve serving God in what looked suspiciously like the wilderness. But I was confident that would soon change. My new husband and I would have a time of hardship, and then move on into success—the kind of spiritual success appropriate for intelligent, educated Christians such as ourselves. If the wilderness is at hand, can the Promised Land be far away? I was ready and eager to go.

In addition, I was making a crucial assumption. Deep down I suspected God had plucked me out of my high-profile, upward-driving music business career in order to deliver some high-profile, upward-driving achievements for him. God apparently needed me for some special project, presently undisclosed.

In the end, I guess I just believed, with the enthusiasm of a new believer, that with God all things are possible. I plunged into the inspiring beautiful spiritual picture of all that I could imagine happening.

So, yes, all that spiritual expectation was now rolled up in this Portland morning as I sat on the edge of another bed (having decided I absolutely must get up or possibly never get up again), in wrinkled pajamas with my hair sticking out.

It wasn't just change. The love of diverse experiences, of learning new things and of taking on challenges has made change from one seemingly unrelated arena to another a personal theme. I could see God had made cunning use of these transitions in my spiritual development. Over and over, God has penetrated my spiritual defenses by using change as the tool.

But this was frightening me. Once again, change was being used to change me, but it felt like getting pulled out of shape. Into shapelessness.

Things had veered off in wildly unexpected directions. When they did, I found myself responding in ways I wasn't used to. Often promising new directions simply vaporized into no direction at all.

The growing realization that I couldn't seem to get this new life on track was wreaking havoc on my attempts to understand what God was doing. After two years in Portland, I felt not only still free-floating, but also increasingly losing any meaningful way to tell myself my own story. The story I had been telling myself on a daily basis to explain the last 30 years of my life was disintegrating.

New insights were piling up. And these more insightful ways of seeing my past were breaking my heart. Three years after my divorce, I was beginning to decide I had done myself in. I had spent my best self meeting others' unhealthy needs, solving problems generated by chaos from the dysfunction of myself and others, working incessantly to control my fears and manage my anxieties, and to simply survive. In that incessant pulling, I used up much of the energy, drive, creativity and accomplishment needed to live up to my vision of who I told myself I "should" be.

After years trying to be "spiritual," to remain committed to a challenging marriage, to run a pioneering mission-oriented business that seemed like a calling—while also trying to prove myself by earning a share of the American dream—I'd just ended up failing. Breaking my own heart.

Granted, these depressive assessments were a bit out of balance with my outward life. I had a good life in Portland. Most important, there were good, substantive and generous people in my life. Irreplaceable people. But inside, I was in real pain. I simply couldn't find the spiritual logic in my life anymore. Nothing felt connected together; I couldn't detect a direction. I was losing the thread of my spiritual story, unable to find the next chapter.

It was like God was no longer invested in my spiritual journey. It seemed God had abandoned me to the good life, like the celebrity who hands his girlfriend his credit card and tells her to go out and buy herself a birthday present. I wasn't starving, my needs were more than met, but God just didn't care about our relationship anymore.

Being a spiritual director, my instinct in most any situation is to ask: Is God in here somewhere? I had started suspecting the answer. But it surprised me. This dark miasma that had been rolling toward me for weeks sure lined up with descriptions of what spirituality writers call a "dark night of the soul." Beyond that, it was very similar to other experiences like this I'd had before.

I used to think that if you had gone through one dark night of the soul, you surely would never have another one. And I'd experienced a protracted dark night before initiating the changes that led to my divorce. When I moved to Portland, I assumed all that was over. I had paid my dues. But this was faulty spiritual logic. Like "book knowledge" that can lead us to think dark nights happening only to mystics or saints or to see them as a spiritual curiosity of the past—for medieval times or ascetics in monasteries. But dark nights of the soul can come to any of us and do come to many of us. They show up in broad daylight, so to speak—in the middle of daily life, in the middle of the so-called ordinary.

It seems to me these tough periods often descend on us when we are poised on the brink of a spiritual growth step. In order to take that step, we are faced with a choice—a choice we need to make and a choice we need to totally own as our own. So, God withdraws.

Watching the rain drip steadily down the windows, I couldn't help asking: where on earth is God? How can God be in this? I had to ask, despite knowing full well that I often end up finding God entirely *not* where I expect to find God. And that always pushes me into rethinking God.

Padding around on the bedroom carpet in my socks, that's what I was doing. Rethinking God. Aware that one of my slippery slopes is the prospect of rethinking God all the way back to my former atheism. But, surely not . . . surely a whole journey I'd seen as a calling set in motion by Christ wasn't going to end badly?

It just seemed so ironic: that this current collapse of my "spiritual self" started 25 years ago in the soaring ecstasy of a classic "conversion experience." What was wrong with that picture? Well . . . nothing. It wasn't really a contradiction. Wandering into the bathroom in a daze, I was starting to "get it." Starting to see that my conversion began the undermining of everything.

Back in 1985, that midnight in Alabama, I thought "conversion" meant the thrilling launch of my amazing new spiritual self. Jesus showed up as a total surprise; it must be for a reason. He must be summoning me to bring the world my talents and gifts (which he was so astute to scoop up). To answer this call, all I had to do was "convert" my current career and achievements over to a "Christian" career. I would start a ministry—a highly successful ministry, of course. In this new round of life, I would achieve and succeed for God. Although I was only vaguely familiar with the Christian scene, no one could help noticing lots of Christians doing that. They were respected and well-known, even rich. Actually, if I worked with intense purity and dedication—who knows—I might become a saint; a famous saint.

Needless to say, that was an erroneous interpretation. In my bliss, I was unaware that my demise was already underway. God was already starting to crack my shell of grandiosity. Calling me into a wilderness of simultaneous change was the first step. God's pressure cooker.

Of course, when Jesus appeared to me he wasn't there to scoop up a treasure chest of talents. He was stopping mercifully by the side of the road to pick up a young woman who desperately needed healing . . . but who was utterly unaware of that fact.

So, this Portland morning 25 years later was the culmination of a long and slow spiritual development. But this was new. It felt like the darkest point—the crisis—in a long illness. The grim hour when you fear the struggling patient who has recovered many times before will, this time, really die.

"Years and years of trying to make things better, make myself better, and make my relationship with God better has added up to a big zero," murmured a whisper inside as I looked blearily in the bathroom mirror. I know that voice; I hear it on a daily basis. It's a voice that doesn't know my name, but it sure does know my pseudonym. This was my false self talking.

My tsunami of spiritual despair was the aftershock from a vicious inner accusation being made by my false self. The accusation was this: that I had finally managed to totally and completely fail "myself"—that is, my *false* self.

The false self is a psychological defense mechanism; a "survival personality" we start developing as children. Psychologists call this behavior a "coping strategy." A child feels neglected, unheard, unloved, unsafe. This happens for various reasons that may be intentional or unintentional on the part of adults in the child's life. Regardless, the child concludes that who she is simply is not enough to deserve being taken care of, listened to, loved, and protected. The child decides she needs to be someone else, another self—a better self. In fact, she may need to become perfect.

All this takes place on the unconscious level. The little toddler just gradually abandons who she really is in favor of this other, safer self. Her truest and deepest potential goes into hiding, unexpressed. Her God-given possibility as a self is not realized. Life and people are too dangerous and uncertain to risk being who she really is.

The false self is fundamentally motivated by fear. Long before I encountered Jesus, these fears had led me into a lifetime of redefining myself and presenting myself in ways I thought would save me from all that frightened me: from being rejected, being abandoned, being discounted, being a disappointment to others, hated, and thrown out. That's why the young woman Jesus appeared to that night in Alabama was ill and in need of healing. But no one had ever told me. In fact, my form of spiritual illness is widely applauded by our culture, which is a great advocate for the false self and supports it at every turn.

The false self hates the true self, which it views as entirely dangerous. After all, the true self might do something so spontaneously alive it would cause a person to be rejected in alarm or distaste by those on hand and making judgments! The true self is oppressed by the false self. It sags under the false self's heavy demands and burdens. Its life can flicker to the point of going out.

But the "spiritual self" disintegrating out from under me was not my true self. It was not a genuine spiritual being. It was a construct I'd cooked up as part of my false self. In fact, it was a key building block of my false self.

The spiritual part of my false self includes my "good" self, my "perfect" self, my "obedient to God's will" self, my "always thinks of others" self, my "dedicated to higher things" self, my "has common sense" self, my "knows when others don't" self, my "always finds the spiritual perspective" self, my "totally devoted to God" self, even my "courteously restrained" self and my "polite and never angry" self. In short, this edifice of "goodness" can be essential to a false self's image as good and perfect—a winning strategy in the survival system the false self has built up over decades of living. Especially in social settings and the world of institutional religion, this socially-approved self had served me well.

In many ways my spiritual life has focused on the ongoing battle back and forth between my false self (ego identity) and my true self (soul identity)—each gaining and losing ground within myself over a period of decades. The true self is a woman's authentic self— it holds her genuine potential; it's her Christ self. I like to think my true self has been winning, that God has been on her side.

But a major transition, a deep loss, a time of crisis is deeply unsettling. The shock can create a strong temptation to give up spiritual gains made and return to hiding in the false self. Instead of reaching forward, we reach back. Deeply rooted structures, defense structures planted in childhood, suddenly look appealing. Old protective patterns promise some degree of security in a currently very insecure world. We try to cram our exploded life back into the old narrow patterns, so our false self can try—once more, with feeling—to win.

For two years, trying to make my way in a new city and build a new life, I had grabbed onto what was left of my false self. Despite Jesus' 25-year program to free me from my false self, I still held allegiance to it as a potent answer to life's problems. I was spiritually vulnerable. The pressure of my divorce and life-upending move exposed this vulnerability.

Actually, I was more than vulnerable. I was in spiritual danger.

Under the unremitting pressure of change and unpredictability and expectations spinning out of control, my false self was in a state of panic. The "self" my false self could most clearly picture to adopt as my current image was the self I was in my career-oriented 30's, just prior to my conversion. It began ordering up new supplies of youth, good looks, inexhaustible energy, incessant smart decisions, and long stretches of years for building a new career and achievements— core essentials for making a culturally successful transition to my new life. Under those demands, I started applying for heavy-duty career jobs, going back to school and doing all the things that would resurrect the former self of my 30's.

But I stumbled. I felt out of sorts trying to quickly pick up that old self-image. I was stressed attempting to meet the demands of who I used to be in my 30's in a fame- and ego-oriented career in the music business. Slowly, I had to admit that this younger self required resources I no longer had. I had to admit she drew her motivations from drives and desires I no longer had. It wasn't working.

Nonetheless, the false self is tenacious. Culture bombards us with the message that the success of the false self is life's most worthwhile goal. Achievement, fame, money, possessions—all are the outward "markers" that convince the world you are, after all, a worthwhile person. I was in a new, unfamiliar environment lacking virtually all the markers by which people evaluated me back in Colorado. Nobody here knew my history or whether I was a credible person or not.

Wandering around my house at an all-time low, accusing myself of being a loser in life's biggest and most important survival project, I saw the achievement, power and control that my newly re-energized false self craved sliding out of reach. And I was deeply afraid I couldn't survive in this new world without it.

During all the years of changes and upheavals, through all the travails of my personal God-appointed wilderness, despite all of Jesus' efforts against this resilient imposter, I had resisted; keeping various degrees of hope alive that my false self would finally be realized.

This led to incessant bargaining. Bargaining with God. Along these lines: if you aren't going to finally give me what I've always wanted, if you're going to let my 25-year dream of following you into spiritual greatness go down the tube, what are you going to give me instead? Bargaining with myself. Along these lines: if I never had the recognition I want, the power I need, the control that would make me feel secure, can I stand simply being "spiritual?" Would it work? Could it ever really be enough—could it ever truly be safe—to simply try to follow Jesus? Do I dare?

I felt especially vulnerable at this point in life, as an older woman when the general cultural flow was much less in my favor. I was anxious and afraid.

Frankly, my first instinct was to figure out a new strategy for getting back to Egypt. Seeing a chance of letting go and risking reality opening into true freedom, I quickly reached out to pick up my bondage again. To come up with some new way to "pull off" my false self's desires. But I couldn't come up with it. I was stuck.

If you can avoid an accounting of this type, it is possible to keep a "magical" hope alive your entire life that you will one day, somehow, live up to the demands of your false self. But remaining on that magical road will eventually drive a woman into bitterness, into victimhood, or into craziness fueled by an ongoing fantasy about who you are or deserve to be. The false self employs multiple strategies to keep this fantasy and its counterfeit hopes alive. When false self dreams are thwarted, yet the woman still grips her false self image and won't let go, then the resulting anger and disappointment can gradually find new life in self-hatred, victimhood, blaming and bitterness. In this foul swamp where no illusion can be released, her true self rots.

I was at a big fork in the road. I abhorred the escape into denial, but was too unnerved to go forward, and no longer had the resources to go back.

I was at a big fork in the road. I abhorred an escape into denial, but was too unnerved to go forward and no longer had the resources to go back.

In his book *Life of the Beloved*, devotional writer Henri Nouwen shows a vivid understanding of this fork. He describes the trap I was setting for myself by my ongoing choice to live in the world, "yielding to its enormous pressures to prove to yourself and to others that you are somebody".

No matter how much we seem to have "proven," Nouwen says, we know deep down we will lose in the end. We're building our life on sand; the shifting foundation of society's approval. Life becomes a long struggle for survival. And living and surviving are not the same. If we really want to live in this world, he maintains, the world itself cannot be the source of our life. "The world and its strategies may help you to survive for a long time," he writes, "but they cannot help you live because the world is not the source even of its own life, let alone yours."

I had to decide whether to live or keep struggling to survive the false self's living death. Basically, that meant hanging on or giving up.

We don't think of the false self as a drug, but the dynamics are very similar. It's something we're addicted to that creates an altered state of consciousness when reality is too hard to take. We may not be an alcoholic or a drug addict, but virtually all of us have a place in our life where our willpower has hit the wall. There's something we simply can't do—or stop doing. The false self is like that. It's that place in your life where you can never satisfy yourself, but you can't stop trying. In my case, I seemed powerless to free myself from the resuscitated grip of my "good girl" self.

The infrastructure of the false self is often some sort of wonderful story about the self—generally about being "perfect" in the way culture sees it or "good" in the way religion sees it. The favorite words of the false self are "more" (I can be more) and "perfect" (next time I'll get it right). You can't win, because no matter how much you do or achieve, the false self will never declare it enough. It's in control. You're out of control. You can't make it come true, and you can't give up trying. You are trapped in the mid-ground of defeat.

Then an extraordinary crisis comes. It blows your house to the ground. It seriously interrupts your story at the core. It can look like chaos. In my case, this crisis was a move into a whole new world at a relatively late point in life. At the high point in life when many people are resting on their laurels and enjoying the fruits of their labors, I was trying to start all over in a totally foreign environment. It was stretching me too far, beyond all my previous limits.

Yet, this excruciating crisis, this seeming chaos, may be the prelude—the necessary condition, even—to God's deliverance. It knocks out the false self's resources and undermines its desires. With all the losses, you no longer could satisfy this oppressive self, even if you wanted to. Beyond that, you gradually . . . gradually . . .start to realize you no longer want to. You start seeing that your false self has been telling you lies.

So, the final blow—the one where you finally break apart into a million tiny little pieces—is the one that may set you free. The final blow may be a form of grace. The grace of finally knowing you are at the end of your resources.

Spiritual writers of great wisdom used to call this shattering blow, "brokenness." Brokenness, being broken, having broken one's own heart—literal shattering—can be the precondition for the surrender into the freedom of a new story.

That's why God allows a crisis, allows things to fall apart, and then sends people into the wilderness where resources are lean. It shatters the old story line. Your old story, grounded in resources you once possessed but no longer have, powered by old motivations you once possessed but no longer have, is in disarray. The plot line is no longer possible. In the wilderness, your story gets broken.

We sometimes need radical discontinuousness in our lives to break our identification with a story the false self has been telling us for a lifetime. The Exodus liberation was not merely about getting the people out of Egypt. Far more importantly, it was about getting the Egypt out of the people.

Compared to the abundance I had imagined before leaving for Portland, my first years there were challenging and lean. Spiritually, I felt cut off from my story—wandering in the wilderness trying to find a new one. That rainy morning when I woke up engulfed in a tsunami of despair and disappointment about "myself"—it was coming. Right in the midst of my lowest ebb, the gift was being given. In reality, the true self cannot be sought but, somehow, in the midst of seeking God, it comes.

Our spiritual task is to allow ourselves to be pulled forward into what looks like death. Then to wait there, reserving judgment, possibly for a long time. Spiritual understanding often only comes in retrospect, after the ending is known. Holding on meanwhile can be an excruciating dimension of faith.

Even as I write this, I still periodically wonder if I am going to be able to overcome the effects of even a small modicum of knowing God. The Bible says no one can see God and live. Entering the 26th year of my spiritual journey, gradually emerging from this most recent dark night of the soul, the truth of that statement increasingly bears down on me.

When reading the Bible I notice that people acquainted with God seem to spend a lot of time in difficult places—down wells, in the desert, in the wilderness, at the bottom of pits. Can you really offer "wisdom" to people undergoing such an experience? Who may be faced with making up their relationship with God as they go along? In such places, the situation and terrain are ever-changing. Sometimes the biggest challenge is just to stay in the game.

So, any advice must be tentative and interim, flexible and adaptable to the moment, yet providing a strong undergirding network of meaning. In places of wilderness, one must become a guerilla fighter. Here are a few of my key guerilla strategies.

Find your Story

Search and search until you find the bigger story that you want your story to be a part of, the deeper story that is more than your own individual, personal story. This is your personal myth that makes sense of your life. This is the battleground of your true and false selves. This is the lifeline, the True North you hold on to.

> "A Story doesn't thread events together like beads on a string, instead it keeps us in thrall by promising us an ending that was there, hiding in the beginning all along. . . . A Story is an expression of how the world matters to us,

and thus interest, passion, caring—fire—thread our time." – David Weinburger

Your story is your source of meaning. This is not false self meaning or cultural meaning, i.e. it is not alien territory. This story is your home base, and it can continually orient you toward "home." Finding the right story to interpret your life is coming home to yourself. It is vitally important that the origin of this story be real and valid.

An old story you've told yourself for a long time can be intimately and complexly intertwined with your false self. One has functioned as the lifeblood of the other—they are "symbiotic," needing the other to survive. It's easy to cling to stories that encode all our sense of entitlement into one hypnotic, entrancing narrative—stories that tell us in detail about what we are due from life, what life owes us, what a person like us should have, in short, all we have decided that life and God has promised us. The disillusionment when that story shatters can be beyond profound.

But beneath every story in which the false self stars in an ego-satisfying drama, there is a more foundational story. This is the true self's story. It is a story of love and deliverance. And it is this story that we must grab on to, to be able to reinterpret our life into a new birth.

True self stories can be found in more than one place. The story of the Exodus and the story of the Cross, perhaps the world's two greatest and most enduring stories of liberation, have profoundly moved and shaped the human race for thousands of years. A personal version combining these two stories is my core story. Tolkien's *Lord of the Rings* trilogy and *The Road* by Cormac McCarthy have also been important to me.

106

In selecting and constructing your story, here are some pointers I've found valuable.

- figure out how it's going to happen and then accept that's not how it's going to happen;
- figure out when you'll be ready to enter the promised land, then add 40 years;
- realize that your story doesn't belong to you; it is your part in a bigger story;
- accept a new story.

Let It All Die (believe in the dark)

If you are a Christian and hear the call to take up your cross, this means dying. Not "sort of" dying or "somewhat" dying or giving up hot fudge sundaes for Lent. We're talking about a spiritual or psychological or physical state analogous to a person hanging on a cross. You can't be resurrected from the dead unless you are dead.

How do you know you're dying? You feel it. How do you know you're dead? You feel dead. Unlike upbeat theologies of consistent faith, this can mean feeling utterly devastated. Wasted and without hope. Abandoned like Jesus on the cross.

How does a busy woman even have time for this to happen? It's happening all around us all the time. It happens to us. Although you are out in the world walking around doing all the things you normally do with a smile on your face, although you have a job and are performing well, although you may appear basically normal even to the people who know you best, you know at the core of your being that something is dying or lying inside you dead. To quote the prophet Ezekiel: "My bones are dried up, and my hope is lost; I am clean cut off." (Ezekiel 37:11b.)

These deaths go on in daily life all around us under the radar of what appears to be "normality."

They are the stuff of transformation happening in our midst when we know only that someone is having a "tough time." Or when we know nothing. We think they are fine. But, interiorly, they are on a cross.

Experiences like this, of myself and others, have revised my view of the role of confusion in the spiritual life. In some religious circles, confusion is viewed as the work of the devil or evil forces. And, certainly, many types of confusion can be very destructive. But chaos theory in science and quantum mechanics shows us that confusion—or radical disorganization—is a fundamental dynamic of the universe. Often things—or a person—must fall into a radical state of confusion and disarray before they become flexible enough to be rebuilt on a new basis. Feeling confused to the point of despair can be a prelude to rebirth; to transformation.

I would urge you, if you really desire God, to allow yourself to be transformed, not merely healed. Healing cycles back around—it returns us to a former state; transformation is the creation of an entirely new state.

A cyclical system, like nature and its cycle of seasons, is based on what I call "hibernation and resuscitation." A cyclical system never actually dies. This, I believe, is one reason we find nature so reassuring—it repeats and repeats the same process without interruption. Death and resurrection is a much, much riskier process. Unlike the continuity of a cycle, it is discontinuous. Something stops, is over. Can it be reborn? Can something greater than what died be born in its place? Maybe. Maybe not. Letting anything die is a risk. Unless you are in the right hands, you know there is a genuine possibility of failure; of total loss. Even Jesus struggled with feeling abandoned as his life apparently failed.

For me, Jesus acquired the credibility to guarantee my faith when he cried out his own feelings of abandonment. He knows what it's like to be unsure that God's plans are working. But he came out of the tomb as the One who can assure me that if I agree to this risk, my true self will emerge. This, as I understand it, is the essence of following Jesus: to trust the road that Jesus took. To trust that, even if I die in every way familiar to me, I will live again.

That is why my heart was broken that morning. My story about myself was dying. And I was struggling to find the faith to believe it would live again.

But the Bible and spiritual saints tell us this is the opening when there's a real chance to win our freedom. When the old self I've always consorted with is dead; when it's burned out of me, I may have a window of escape. A chance to fly out and center my life around the Living One instead of the False One; to start drawing my life from that Center. To become fully alive.

Hang on to your friends. (and family members who are friends)

Without friends, companions, a small community of people who love me, I believe I would be literally dead. I have felt suicidal, as my divorce recovery workshop predicted. I have felt God was pushing me too far. In the grandiosity of my false self, I have pushed myself too far. You need a few faithful friends who will stand at the foot of your cross when you feel dead, even if you aren't.

Don't withdraw from them to conserve energy. You can spend your energy in no better way. Accept help. You can return it later. When I've fallen into those crucial points of transformation—situations that seemed like "mini-deaths," a dark night of the soul—

my friends are the ones who've saved me from more God than I could handle.

They come in and pick up the lifeless body. They take it to the tomb where it can lay quietly, giving it time to come alive while it has all the appearance of decomposing.

One day you get up, throw off the rotten bindings, and try again. Your friends bring you chicken soup and fresh bread. You eat heartily and get ready to move on. Because you can't go back. By then God has barred the way back, has cut off all roads that lead back to Egypt.

Your friends are your "soul eyes" who help you see your life when you can't. Who understand what it is telling you. Day after day, I kept seeing a horrifying vision of my whole life burning. Every minute from birth until present was spread out on a vast plain and engulfed in a raging prairie fire: burning down to blackened stubble, my life a ruin. It was my friend, gifted with a Native American background, who quietly listened into my horror and said, "But, Lola, prairie fires are so hot, they release the seeds that are never able to otherwise grow."

Learn to Manage your Freedom All Over Again

After a long process when the false self's protective shell has been loosened and loosened and then a layer or two drops away, you're . . . much more free. The image is that you soar away like a beautiful butterfly. But new freedom can be terrifying freedom.

You can drown in the silence and stillness of your new freedom as the incessant buzzing and bondage of your old story fades. The temptation to take up the old self and its busy ways returns in force in this scary silence. Like the very Godself, a new level of freedom can evoke joy, awe—and sheer terror.

When reborn at some level, it can seem like being a teenager again. In your new liberty, you're learning to manage freedom, real freedom, for the first time. It requires learning to create our own structure from within. Normally our lives are incredibly determined, structured, scheduled. We heavily rely on this structure and on our preoccupation with the false self's many projects. We take for granted that this is who we are.

Letting go of the externally imposed structure of the false self can feel premature, like we aren't ready. And suddenly, we don't know who we are; the true self is still young an inexperienced. Entering the Promised Land means starting over and learning to manage freedom when there's a whole slate of new choices and no tyrant telling you what to do.

Risk Some Risks

Fundamentally, the false self is built on compliance—it's all about conforming to what other people want. In this sense, it is impossible for the false self to serve God. It's too busy serving other people in your life. It's too busy serving your idea of who you need to be to gain their approval.

Becoming more "spiritual" would seem to simply mean becoming increasingly more aligned with the Spirit. In this sense, becoming spiritual (i.e. moving toward God) is actually an act of extreme resistance, as opposed to continued compliance.

Formerly a slave to your image, you were genuinely "conservative"—always trying to conserve and protect the self and the self's image. That image was your guiding vision. Now you are free to take risks in the service of a bigger vision. The false self has counterfeit dreams. It promises you the moon and gives you moldy cheese.

The true self is genuine dreaming. It dreams dreams worth the risk—worth a willingness to fly too close to the sun. If you are ever going to fly, the time is now—don't pull in your wings.

Due to God's timing, I have ended up writing this essay when a long-known form of myself has recently passed away, and I am still near the vortex of grief. But some grief is pure grief, welcome grief, clean grief, grief for that whose time is rightly over.

My self has started springing back in new ways. It's not the life put together out of old habits of being that I anticipated when driving my trusty Jeep out to Portland. Instead, more primitive dreams that the false self began pushing aside as early as age six have begun floating into view, coming back into focus.

God has extended my storyline both backward and forward. Daily I more clearly see that God's promises to me didn't start with my conversion experience; they started with my birth. Focusing on my life since that one experience cuts my story short and compresses God's promises onto narrow horizons. The wider, longer, deeper promises that began at my birth are resilient enough to carry my story into the future. They are sturdy enough to support the repeated risk that living a new story requires.

Moving forward and exploring more authentic ways of being has taken me back into important things I'd forgotten about myself, into talents and passions that had been put on the shelf. God knocks them off the shelf. I pick them up and dust them off. Examine them. Some still look real.

God's way of coming at things is so unexpected, so creative, I can hardly take it in. Even though I recognize this truer self when I see her, I still have trouble easily calling her "my life." But, one day at a time, I am learning how to say my true name.

Put the Key in the Ignition

by Marilyn Kirvin

ONE

I SIT in the small examining room holding my breath, as the surgeon, Dr. A, runs his fingers over my neck. He finishes, and says to me, "I can certainly feel the lump, and the C-T scan tells us that something is definitely there. Since this is the third time that the thyroid cancer has returned, I think it's pretty clear that this cancer has changed—we thought it was papillary cancer, but I think it's behaving much more like anaplastic thyroid cancer." He pauses, but my expression must tell him that I know what this means, because he continues, "We will do a biopsy, and I'll call you with the results." Then, "Are you ok? Is there anything we can do for you?" I tell him I'm fine, and I quickly make my way out of his office. Almost an hour later I call my friend John in Seattle, "I'm in the parking garage at my doctor's office. He told me I probably have anaplastic cancer . . . the kind that only gives me six months to live. I've been sitting here for 45 minutes and I don't know what to do." Quietly he says, *"Put the key in the ignition and drive home. We'll figure it out from there."*

As it turned out, the biopsy results indicated that I did not have this more lethal form of cancer, but the papillary cancer that I did have was behaving aggressively, growing quickly and threateningly. I was referred to a doctor at Oregon Health Sciences University who was a specialist in complicated head and neck surgeries.

Dr. G. was a man whose air of quiet authority invited confidence. He told me that I would need a laryngectomy, a surgery that would result in my losing my voice box, and said that I would have to learn to speak in some alternate way. The surgery might involve having to replace my carotid artery with another vein because the tumor was wrapped around it. Although the operation was certainly a risky one, Dr. G. said that, because I was relatively young and had children, he would recommend my doing it because I would be given a chance to live, while not having the surgery would surely result in my death within a few months. I am sure he told me more details, but my mind had fixed on one thing: *I'm going to lose my voice?*

Over the next few weeks I struggled to decide whether to have the operation. Foremost in my mind was the fact that I was the single mother of two teenage sons, which should have made my decision easy: my children needed a mother. But it was almost impossible for me to imagine what my life would be like without a voice.

My work was to give retreats and accompany people as a spiritual director—everything I did involved speaking, so how would I support my family? And beyond that, I wondered whether people (including my sons) would accept me with this disability. There were moments when I came close to saying I could not do it, but in the end what was clearer to me than anything was that what my sons wanted was to have their mother with them—even a mother with a strange voice. And although I was, at times, overwhelmed with uncertainty and fear, I wanted to be there too. I wanted to have the chance to dance at their weddings and hold my future grandchildren. And so we scheduled the surgery.

In the month leading up to the surgery I worked hard to prepare for every possible outcome. Along with my family and friends, I hoped for a miracle—hoped that somehow the doctors would be wrong and my voice would be preserved. But I knew that my real work was to both be willing to let go of my life, if it came to that, and also (in some ways, this was the harder challenge) to say yes to living this new life, a life I just wasn't sure I wanted. As part of this process of preparation I made sure to say things that I knew needed to be said while I still could—words of forgiveness, of challenge, and especially of love. I even made a 45-minute recording for my teenage sons, telling stories of their lives, reading from books from their childhoods, letting them hear, in my natural voice, how much they meant to me.

Throughout all of this time, whenever fear about the future washed over me, John's words would come back: *put the keys in the ignition and drive home, and we'll figure it out from there.* Take the next step, do the next thing, trust that you are not doing this alone. Even in my fear I had a sense of being guided, a sense that God was somehow present in all that was unfolding.

However, that sense of presence went away as soon as I checked into the hospital. Later—much later—the words of a friend who had survived a brain tumor helped me to make sense of what I experienced: *"For me, one of the hardest parts was feeling the loss of spirit after surgery. The anesthesia and pain medication and the huge strain on the body*

115

in general causes the spirit to fly away somewhere.
There are weeks and weeks, if not months of sheer
survival when nothing is felt at all." It would be a
long time before I would feel my spirit starting to
return. And yet, as painful as this sense of loss was,
there was also great grace...but grace known mostly in
retrospect

Two

I wake up in the Intensive Care Unit and realize
two things fairly quickly: I am alive, and my voice
is gone. There has been no miracle. But I also see
that Susie and Dave are standing at my bedside.
My sister Susie has taken a three-week leave from
her job as a teacher in Arvada, Colorado, to stay
with me. Meanwhile, Dave has come from Las
Vegas for a day or two, leaving behind his own
family and his successful Public Relations firm to
support both of his sisters and be with his
nephews. The night before the surgery we had all
gone out to dinner and, as is so typical with our
family, Susie and I kidded our "little brother"
mercilessly about his discomfort with all the
ickiness—the germs and blood—associated with
illness. Later, we asked each other whether he
would be able to handle being at the hospital. But
now, as I open my eyes in the ICU, he is here. As I
lie stitched and swollen, covered in bandages,
tubes and drains drawing all manner of bodily
fluids from me, my brother stands beside
me, talking, joking, and never once turning away.

That experience, of one willing to stand with me
in my suffering, was a gift of presence that I received
over and over again. The gift was not about fixing or
even changing the situation. It was about being in the

midst of it with me. During my 31 days at OHSU it came whenever Susie, or John, or my sister-in-law Brigette sat (and sometimes slept) in my room so that I would not be alone. It was given when my sons came to visit me, and acted as though everything was normal in our very precarious and decidedly un-normal world. These moments of presence in the midst of pain were my introduction to the God who was to be with me throughout this new time of my life.

And the gift of presence was not just found through my family: it was bestowed whenever there was some human connection with one of the resident doctors, or when a nursing assistant offered to wash my hair (no easy task in my condition). It was also given when Andrew, the speech language pathologist, challenged me-kindly, but firmly - to use the artificial speech device that I hated, and so taught me that tough-love feels much more supportive when delivered in a British accent. And the gift of presence came in moments of humor, as when I finally left my hospital floor after a month, wearing my green velour bathrobe, to have lunch in the cafeteria, and ran into Dr. G., who broke into a surprised smile and said, "Maybe we should be thinking about you going home." Only now, looking back, do I sense that I was being constantly, quietly, urged back into the land of the living through the care and love of all of these witnesses, incarnations of that mysterious Divine energy, moving us along.

Two weeks after I was discharged from OHSU I flew to Colorado to live with Susie as I underwent radiation treatments. While I was there I was remarkably fortunate to be cared for by some compassionate and gifted medical personnel. But the central witness to this part of my journey, the one whose presence allowed my spirit to survive some very dis-spiriting moments, was my sister. Opening her home to me (the home in which we had grown up), she turned her schedule upside down to care for me during the next five months – months that included an unexpected return to Portland for a second surgery, and a series of complications emerging from radiation that resulted in multiple trips to doctors' offices and emergency rooms. Susie was a gifted organizer and my unfailing cheerleader through all those months, but I also caught glimpses of how painful it was for her to watch me go through all that this time entailed; but watch she did, faithfully, constantly, like a sentinel guarding me from cruel and foolish people, willing to take the arrows, but not to let me be hurt. I loved her for that, and knew that her presence alone gave me strength and comfort, grounding me in safety in the midst of so much chaos.

THREE

I walk into the radiation treatment room, where the technician is preparing for my appointment. She asks me, "Is this your photo on the computer screen? What is your birth date? What are we treating?" I have heard the same questions every day, always the same. In answer to the last one I swipe my hand across my throat and we both smile. I lie down on the platform, and the technician brings over the large, mesh-like mask that encases my face and neck to hold me still and to direct the beams of radiation. She bolts the mask to the platform so that I am unable to move or to see. A surge of panic, always my first response, rises up; but then I start to breathe, in and out. I recall the mantra from Michael Brown's book, *The Presence Process: "I am, here now, in this."* I lie there breathing and the calm rises in me.

I am here. God is here. God is only here, in this moment. I am safe.

I hated radiation . . . every moment: from walking through the door to changing into the gown; from sitting in the waiting room with my fellow patients to feeling my head bolted down again in this act that would send even non-claustrophobes into a panic. And perhaps fittingly, this daily ritual became a symbol for me of my larger spiritual struggle.

I did not want to be doing radiation, with all of the resulting exhaustion and nausea. I did not want to have this cancer. I did not want to be without a voice. Inside I felt I was screaming and no one could hear. I wanted it all to end and I could tell no one. It wasn't that I wanted to die, I just wanted . . . well, I suppose I wanted my old life back. And I wanted to *feel* God was there

During this time my friend Norine sent me an essay by Brian Doyle. It told how the Virgin Mary came to him one night at a very difficult time in his life. She said to him, "Let it go." These words transformed him and his experience. A few nights after reading this essay, I woke from a sound sleep absolutely furious, and said to the darkness, "Fine, so show up! Tell me to 'let it go.' Or tell me 'go to sleep,' like you said to Elizabeth Gilbert in *Eat, Pray, Love.* Just tell me something!" I sat there for several minutes, yet I heard nothing except the hiss of the humidifier and the sound of my own breathing.

Grief, pain, silence . . . I kept waiting for the epiphany, the moment of enlightenment, and yet it never came. What came instead were moments, moments like shards of glass that would pierce the silence and the fear—not always comforting, but somehow true—moments of a God who was here, now. Whether on that radiation table, or when I was nauseated, exhausted, or wondering if I should just give it up, I was stabbed by this conviction of God's presence. In those times it brought no happiness or warmth but simply goaded me, keeping me going. When I could remember that God was here, only here, only now, the fears of my future, or the questions of how much more I could handle, disappeared. The sharp edge of presence meant I could live through this moment, and then the next, and the next, and the next. It was all that I was given. As it turned out, it was enough.

FOUR

It's early February, and I have three more weeks until the end of radiation. Several friends have offered to visit me in Colorado, but I have asked them not to—I am spent and know that I will not have the energy to act as host. Then John announces that he will be arriving in Denver in a week. I ask (or more accurately, *beg)* him not to come, and tell him that I just don't have it in me to be present to him. My sister, who has come to know John well, says, "Go ahead and tell him not to come, but John is going to do what John wants to do." His flight lands at 4 on a Friday afternoon.

For five days we do little else but sit on Susie's couch and watch television—*Law and Order* reruns, old movies, whatever is on. Only once do we have a real conversation about our lives and all that is happening. And occasionally, as we sit there, John simply holds my hand. After about a day and a half, I start to feel it—as though something that is frozen in the middle of me is thawing, as if I am remembering who I am, and that I am not alone. So different from the hard grace of the radiation room and the doctor's office, this experience was just as true and important, though in a different way.

That experience with John, that sense of life coming through the simple act of another human being holding my hand, reminded me of Parker Palmer's story of his time of deep depression, when the one person who reached him was the man who came to visit him at 4 p.m. every day and, without saying a word, simply massaged his feet. Now I understood that story in a much deeper way.

It wasn't just John, of course. It was Susie. It was my sons—Matt's text messages every other day ("Hey, how are you doing?"), and Andrew's stained glass butterfly with the note: "This is to remind you that you are in a cocoon now, but you'll be coming back to us a butterfly." It was Brigette sending us flowers and chocolate on every holiday. It was the neighbors on Flower Street who had known me since I was nine and who would stop by just to say hello. It was the hundreds of messages on my CaringBridge website from every part of my life. It was all the cards and little gifts, including, one day, a set of Valentines From God, made by a woman I barely knew. It was so much, and I often felt as though this web of relationships held me into being, even when *I* wanted to let go.

FIVE

Radiation has been over for a couple of weeks, and I am walking, slowly, along a path at a nature preserve not far from Susie's house. The day is cloudy and blustery. As I walk my mind is blustery too. I think how I will need to go back home to Portland soon. I worry about whether I will be able to care for myself. I think of my body, the chronic pain, the constant ache of walking, the breath so hard to come by. Will it always be this way? I wonder about the cancer: is it gone? Will it return? The shadows grow long. Suddenly the thought comes again: *If this is what is happening, then God must be here.* My trance of anxiety has been broken, and I am awake. And now as I walk, I see the land around me, the geese flying, the first signs of spring in tulips breaking through the hard ground. God is only here, only now.

Six

It is mid-May. I have been home now for 3 weeks, going almost daily to doctors, trying to organize my life after having been apart from it for seven months. Yet, even with so much to do, I feel a need for some time just to be. I decide to take a week alone at the Oregon Coast, staying at the home of my friends Jane and George. I tell people I am going there to give my spirit a chance to return to me. But it is not an easy retreat. As I walk through town, or on the beach, places I have loved visiting for 15 years, the constant awareness of my body— its pain and discomfort—frustrates me, as though I am standing in my own way, keeping myself from seeing all that is around me. I want things to be back the way they once were.

I write to John, saying that I am grateful for all the ways that God has been with me, but that I still find myself asking God, "Where *are* you?" John responds, "*Maybe you should let go of all those things you think you're supposed to feel, and just let yourself feel. Then you can see if God actually does show up where you are."* When I hear this, it bothers me because it seems so obvious—but I start to write in my journal anyway, letting all the feelings of these months spill out . . . anger and grief, even despair. Again, I get no answers, and nothing in my situation changes. But when I finish writing, I realize that the depth of desire for connection with God *is* the presence of God. God is here. The next day as I walk the beach I notice I am smiling. I am not thinking of my body. Instead, I am seeing the waves roll in and the gulls fly by. Something is different, and I am grateful.

I waited to finish this essay until my time at the beach; part of me hoping for some revelation, some enlightenment that a retreat might provide. None came. What I got instead was time and quiet to realize that life is not about reaching Happily Ever After, as tempting as that seems. There is no place of perfect insight, perfect peace, perfect faith where, once we reach it, we will stay forever in safety.

Rather, life is joy and suffering unfolding step by step. The gratitude of the beach is followed by the sorrow of the highway home, and then that is followed by the joy of seeing loved ones again and telling them the story. God is found in our life as it is. And our call is to live, to be present to our lives, in pain or in promise, and sometimes in both.

Let It Go
Let go of the ways you thought life
would unfold; the holding of plans
or dreams or expectations—Let it
all go. Save your strength to swim
with the tide. The choice to fight
what is here before you now will
only result in struggle, fear, and

desperate attempts to flee from the
very energy you long for. Let go.
Let it all go and flow with the grace
that washes through your days whether
you receive it gently or with all your
quills raised to defend against invaders.
Take this on faith: the mind may never
find the explanations that it seeks, but
you will move forward nonetheless.
Let go, and the wave's crest will carry
you to unknown shores, beyond your
wildest dreams or destinations. Let it
all go and find the place of rest and
peace, and certain transformation.

© Danna Fauld
from *Go In and In*

Goodbye, Again

by Gale Cunningham

And we know that all things work together for good to them that love God, to them that are called according to his purpose.
— Romans 8:28

THE THREAT of freezing fog hung heavily in the air as my 13-year-old-son JR and I climbed into the car for yet another two-hour drive from our Portland home to Eugene. This was the third trip in the last week to see JR's dying father.

It was January 20th, 1994, seven months almost to the day, since the devastating diagnosis. The words "fourth-stage renal cell carcinoma" echoed through my mind, as I slid into the driver's seat to warm up the engine. I had first heard them on June 19th of the previous year. Instead of celebrating his 45th birthday, my former husband called us with a bombshell: the worsening pain he had first noticed in his back and legs while golfing was actually end-stage kidney cancer. He was given six months to live.

John had quit his three-pack-a-day smoking habit and waged a tough battle, enduring agonizing chemotherapy and experimental treatments, determined to beat the disease. But now, cancer was beating him. John had gotten markedly worse in the last two weeks and was slipping, fast. The hospice nurse said he might last another 24 hours—or not. I hadn't yet wrapped my mind around it, let alone my heart, and I could only imagine what JR must be feeling. A reticent soul by nature and having just become a teenager, he wasn't about to confide in his mother.

"Buckle up," I reminded my son, as I started backing out of the driveway.

"I GOT it, Mom," he snapped, settling into the front passenger seat and firmly clamping his Walkman headset over his ears, as if to drown out the gravity of the situation.

Culture Club's "Karma Chameleon" blasted from JR's headphones as I steered the car east toward Interstate-205. It was 5:30 p.m. and darkness had already fallen. I dreaded this drive as much because of the frigid forecast, as the purpose of the trip. The northwest was caught in a cold snap, and I knew that driving conditions would be especially treacherous through the heart of the Willamette Valley, between Salem and Eugene.

I had leaned on and grown in my Catholic Christian faith over these last very difficult months. Not only was my son's father dying, I had lost my job and my second marriage of two years was crumbling, along with my self esteem. I might have lost it altogether, if not for a close and loving friend who chose to reveal his protection and care for me in very poignant ways during that period of my life. There were times when it seemed Jesus was the only one who understood the painful hurdles I faced.

My current husband Matt had refused to make this trip, nursing a dark, sullen jealousy that had festered with John's illness. Just before we left the house that evening, he had exploded.

"You love HIM more than me! I hope you're both miserable as hell, and by the way, I wouldn't miss you if something happened and you didn't come home tonight," he hissed.

Emotionally raw, I had w-a-a-a-a-y too much on my plate to deal with Matt's issues now, I thought as I drove. I was focused on getting JR through the next few days. Turning onto the freeway on-ramp, I asked again silently for help. "Lord, please ride with us. Get us safely to Eugene in time to see John before you take him home. Thank you."

When I pulled off at Gladstone, a few miles down the freeway, to gas up, I decided to call my Aunt Dee and Uncle Bill in Sublimity. It was Sunday, a school night for JR, and their home half-way between Eugene and Portland was a safe haven from which we could easily drive on to school in the morning. Dee and Bill's door was always open to guests, especially loved ones, a hospitality they had extended to John even after the divorce. They had visited him while he was sick, and they shared our grief. Yes, they would welcome our brief visit.

Back on the road again, my mind took a trip of its own, revisiting the last 18 good, bad and ugly years I had shared with John, spanning our courtship and marriage, the abuse, JR's birth, John's infidelity and, ultimately, the end of our marriage.

I was a 22-year-old wide-eyed cub reporter and he the more seasoned journalist, when we met at work early in 1976. I fell in love with the deep, golden voice I heard on the radio, but I found John to be very different from the image in my mind's eye. He was nice looking, but physically imposing at nearly six-feet-four-inches tall, with a head of thick, half-gray hair that aged him beyond his 27 years. He also had an intimidating air about him and a short fuse—he'd been known to throw things at work if he got frustrated enough.

Looking back, that should have been enough to send me running in the other direction. But as we started working together, John softened. He was brilliant, had a charming, Midwestern-style wit laced with infectious laughter, he was a Christian and we shared similar family backgrounds. Soon, he asked me for a date and it wasn't long before we became an item. After our third date, he sent me flowers, with a hand-written poem tucked inside, declaring his feelings. We married a year and a half later.

Following a wonderful wedding celebration, John and I soon settled into what I expected would be a stable, happy marriage. I couldn't have been more wrong. I would come to know John as a walking contradiction: the tender poet who often wore his heart on his sleeve was also capable of exploding in a blind rage, as if possessed by the devil himself. Our relationship spiraled into a cycle of abuse that sent me to the hospital on at least one occasion.

Just after our first wedding anniversary, my parents and Bill and Dee suggested that John and I attend a Marriage Encounter weekend. John reluctantly agreed and the communication tools we learned transformed our relationship—for awhile. We resumed going to church after a long absence, and John, raised in the Presbyterian tradition, decided to become a Catholic. We made new friends with Marriage Encounter couples, and it was about this time that Mom and Dad introduced us to Tom and Susan, who had been on their Encounter weekend. I remembered admiring Susan's long, perfectly-manicured fingernails and how I'd mentally chastised myself for sensing that she wouldn't hesitate to use them on *me*! Still, we'd become friends. But others would later tell me they had noticed Susan's inordinate interest in John from the get-go.

"Mom, I'm thirsty" JR pleaded, interrupting my walk down memory lane. "Can we stop for something to drink?"

We were now on Interstate-5 in Salem, where fog was beginning to wrap everything in a shroud of white, and ice crystals sparkled on the freeway. We quickly hit a McDonald's for pop and coffee, before cautiously resuming the trip south to Eugene, the fog getting thicker by the second.

We had barely gone a mile when I had a "Moses" moment. Suddenly, the freezing fog parted, revealing a clear, dry road ahead. My prayer answered, I released my white-knuckle grip on the wheel and relaxed for the final hour of the drive. My mind traveled back in time once more.

John morphed into a Doctor Jekyll/Mr. Hyde; I never knew which I was dealing with. Marriage counseling had been of little help, and we separated more than once. Still, in a calm period marked by the absence of more physical violence, we decided to start the family John and I had always wanted. JR, the light of my life, was born in November of 1980.

Sadly, that didn't keep John's behavior from escalating. At one point, he threatened to kill me, but I could not shake my Catholic upbringing that forbade divorce. I stood firmly by my man, hoping he would change, the words "to love, honor and cherish until death do us part" ringing through my head. It never occurred to me that there are many kinds of death— including the death of a marriage. Realizing how dangerous the situation had become, a worried friend urged me to speak with the pastor at a Catholic parish in the West Hills. He explained that it was not God's plan for my son and me to endure abuse. With his reassurance that, in fact, God expected me to protect my child, I made the decision I'd been avoiding.

I'd come a long way in my thinking, but my resolve was put to the test a few days later, when John slapped the baby. Now eight months old, JR was fussy from teething, and it was Mr. Hyde who bolted from his chair and hit him in the face with a deck of cards, spewing profanities and yelling for me to put the baby in his crib. I locked myself and my terrified son in his room. I calmed JR enough to feed him and put him to bed. Then, before falling into a fitful sleep in the rocking chair, I made plans to leave—and I knew it had to be for the last time. Our marriage of four years had to end before something tragic happened.

The following morning, after John went to work, I packed up JR and moved to a friend's house on the other side of town. I called Susan to let her know what was happening. She had news of her own: she and Tom were separating, as well. I commiserated with my friend, completely unaware of the subterfuge in play.

A month later, the Friday before our first divorce hearing, John came to see me, wanting to reconcile. I laid out my terms: in-patient psychiatric evaluation and treatment, followed by more marriage counseling. He said he'd think it over. I never heard from him again.

A few days later, I learned that John had moved Susan into *our* home the day after that conversation. I would find out later that that they had been seeing each other for some time.

"For he will command his angels concerning you, to guard you in all your ways." — Psalm 91:11

After a year-long court battle, I was awarded sole custody of our son. Once the divorce was final, I returned to that church to thank the priest for his support and guidance in helping me to make such a grave decision. When I arrived asking to see him, the secretary said she had never heard of him. As it happened, there was no record of him at the Archdiocese of Portland, either!

John and Susan lived together for several years, before marrying. JR had never known life with his Dad and us together, as a family, so when John got very ill, I thought it important for him to see some caring between his parents. "Fake it 'til you make it," or, "act as if" became my mantra and a genuine affection returned, as I found myself helping John walk his path. Often when JR and I would visit, Susan would disappear for a couple of hours or more, leaving the three of us alone. In her absence, I learned to change chemo infusion bags and dressings and to just be there. I held John when he wept, frightened of what was to come, prayed with him and even laughed with him again. At times, it almost felt as if we had never parted. I began to wonder if this was the proper role for the spouse-once-removed. I was overwhelmed with conflicting feelings; discernment eluded me. Perhaps God was trying to teach me that there are many kinds of love. I do know God was blessing me with the grace and strength to keep part of a vow that I believed to be hopelessly broken.

When we had visited John just a few days earlier he was thinner, weaker and relied on a cane to walk. He was also very depressed, despite a house full of well-meaning family and friends. Knowing how much he loved baseball, I suggested he watch *The Sandlot*, a recent movie about a boy's summer baseball adventures in a new neighborhood. John got up from his recliner and slowly moved to the chair at his desk, situated against the wall between the family room and kitchen. I followed, sitting in a chair facing him. As John struggled to write the movie information in his

Day Timer, my eyes wandered over his shoulder into the kitchen, where Susan and Paul, John's best friend from back home, were dancing and kissing! I sat stunned, until a tap on the knee brought my eyes to meet John's. They told me that he knew what I was seeing, but what could he do?

As JR and I got ready to start back to Portland later that day, John had insisted on walking us outside to the car, with the help of his father. Reaching the driveway, he asked his dad to leave us alone for a moment. John dropped his cane, hugging JR and me close. "I love you both," he whispered, tears streaming down his face. He held us so tightly, I thought my ribs would break; my heart *did*. I sobbed all the way home.

"Therefore, since we are surrounded by so great a cloud of witnesses, let us rid ourselves of every burden and sin that clings to us and persevere in running the race that lies before us." — Hebrews 12:1

It had only been a few days since that visit and this one would be our last. The car clock read 7:30 p.m., as we finally pulled into the driveway of John and Susan's home. "We're here," I announced, shaking a sleepy JR awake. John's Dad and sisters greeted us at the front door, advising that he was drifting in and out of consciousness, but determined to see us. By the flickering light of the fireplace in the living room to the left of the entryway, my eye caught sight of the hospital bed, with John's now-emaciated frame huddled silently under the covers. "This *is really* happening," I said to myself, hoping that John would sit up and greet us, as he always did. But it was not to be. I realized at that moment there would be no cure; God had tested John in the fire of disease and was ready to take him home.

The soft strains of Jon Secada wafted from the stereo as tears filled my eyes once more. I told JR I would leave him to talk with his dad alone. After a few minutes, JR wandered into the dining room, where I sat talking with John's family. "Dad wants to see *you*," he sighed, slumping into the chair next to me.

I took a deep breath, got up and tip-toed into the softly-lit living room, which I now sensed to be quite crowded, despite the fact that John and I were all alone. This was sacred ground, and I wasn't at all sure what to do or say. I found myself wondering why there was no etiquette book for this sort of thing.

I sat down in a chair beside John's bed, and took his frail left hand. John opened his eyes, trying to focus as he attempted to speak, his once-booming, golden voice failing him. He gripped my hand, struggling to raise his head off the pillow to look into my eyes.

"I'm s-sor-ry," he finally pleaded, "for-give me?"

"I forgave you long ago," I replied tearfully, stroking what little remained of his once-thick hair.

John relaxed back on the pillow again, a slight smile crossing his lips.

"It won't be long now," I whispered, "until Jesus comes to take you to Heaven, where will be no more pain, sorrow or tears, only happiness and love. But, please don't forget us when you get there. JR needs you, and I can't do this alone. I'm counting on you as his father to help me get him to adulthood and watch over him in a way you could never do here; promise me," I begged.

John nodded, closing his eyes in a wince. The pain was back.

"Do you need more meds?" I asked, just as his youngest sister Janet appeared with another dose of morphine.

John managed to tease her as she tenderly administered the needed relief. Within a couple of minutes, he was resting comfortably again, eyes closed. The rest of the family soon joined JR and me at his bedside, where, laying hands on John, we prayed the Lord's Prayer and talked for a few more minutes before it was time to go. John's family left the three of us alone for one last time. JR told his dad he loved him and quickly left the room.

I bent down, took John's hand again, and kissed his forehead. "You will always hold a special place in my heart," I assured him. Tears glistened on his cheeks as he tried to squeeze my hand and mouthed, "bye."

JR was silent, and I cried for the hour it took us to drive to Sublimity, where we would find comfort and a bed for the night.

Back home in Portland the following evening, JR called to Eugene to check on his dad. JR's grandfather broke the news that John had passed peacefully two hours before. JR handed the phone to me and left the room in tears. For John, the long, painful journey was finally over—and our lives forever changed.

Four days later, on January 25th, we gathered at St. Paul's Catholic Church for John's memorial Mass. It was a dark, foreboding winter afternoon; its bitter-cold wind preserving a trace of ice on Eugene's streets, sidewalks and yards.

A lump of anger rose in my throat, as I watched Susan in the foyer, soaking up the attention and sympathy of friends, family and John's professional associates like a dry, thirsty sponge. It was all about her. "How *dare* she?" I seethed to myself, "after all the deceit and betrayal of her dying husband . . . the husband she stole from me . . ."

Suddenly, a voice pulled me from the quicksand of self-pity. "Gale, do you remember me?" I turned around, and there stood a college friend of John's whom I hadn't seen since well before John and I had divorced more than a dozen years earlier.

"Jim, of course I remember you" I smiled, "it's so good to see you again." We spent a couple of minutes catching up on each other's lives, before he offered a surprisingly insightful bit of empathy.

"I am so sorry for your loss," Jim said.

"*M-m-m-y* loss?" I stammered.

He continued, "It must be hard, watching everyone offer sympathies to Susan. You've lost more than she has: not only are you saying goodbye to John all over again, you've also lost your son's father. I just want you to know I am so very sorry."

I managed to blurt out a surprised "Thank you," as the priest signaled it was time to begin the procession into the church.

JR and I followed the rest of John's family up the center aisle, to the front of the church. It was a modern structure, fashioned of brick, wood and glass, artfully designed in a semi-circle, almost-auditorium style. Nearing the front, I whispered to my son that he should sit with the rest of his dad's family toward the center aisle, while I would sit off to the side.

"No Mom," JR insisted, "I'd rather sit with you." So we made our way to our seats at the end of the family pew on the right side of the church.

The Mass proceeded, with Bible readings, a homily, and Communion. The priest delivered the eulogy, mentioning John's 'loving wife' Susan and every one of his surviving family members by name, except his son. JR turned to me, his eyes full of questions I had no answers for. John's wife and family had cruelly excluded him!

The service continued with personal tributes, ending with a musical video of John's life, before someone approached the altar to let Father know that

John's only son was in the church. He rushed to correct the omission, apologizing profusely from the pulpit, but the damage was done. Now, I was left to pass one of the most valuable truths I learned from my parents, to my son: sometimes this life isn't fair.

I pulled JR closer with the final blessing of John's ashes, listening numbly as the priest's invocation faded into the background. My thoughts drifted to the Catholic doctrine on the Communion of Saints, that spiritual solidarity uniting the faithful on earth with Jesus and those who have gone on ahead of us, in a bond of prayerful support that death cannot break.

Could it be?

Suddenly, a blinding light pierced the thick, black sky on the right side of the building, as though tearing through the thin veil separating this world from the next. With laser-like precision, the bright sunbeam shot through one pane of the bank of windows on the wall above us and came to rest on JR and me, bathing just the two of us in its warm spotlight.

"This is Not What I Expected!"

by Marilyn Jaeger Veomett

I WATCHED as my typically calm and collected daughter blurted these words and looked at her new son with complete astonishment on her face. A few minutes earlier, she and her husband had just met their second adopted child—a beautiful Chinese boy.

In September 2010, my husband George and I travelled to China with our oldest daughter, her husband and their 3-year-old daughter. The five of us were going to meet their second adopted child. We knew a few things about this child. He was about 21 months old. He had lived in an orphanage since he was abandoned at 4 months of age. He had a congenital disability that resulted in the shortening of his left calf and an incomplete left ankle and foot. We had expected that he might be a bit shy and quiet, would likely be somewhat behind developmentally, and that he would be limited in his mobility. We were wrong on all counts!

As our son-in-law held this eagerly awaited new family member, it became clear that he was an extraordinarily strong child, physically strong and strong-willed. His flailing body and his loud, demanding cries were unmistakable evidence of his inner and outer strength. We soon learned that he walked well despite a limp and could easily outrun both George and me. His energy level and his clear demands over the next few days led us to describe him as a combination of the Energizer Bunny and King Tut.

Like many children, whether we give birth to them or adopt them, this child was different than his parents had expected. As our daughter and son-in-law welcomed their new son into their family, they realized very concretely that their family life from now on was going to be different from what they had expected.

As George and I witnessed our daughter's initial shock at her son's strength and intensity, our response was a smile and knowing glance sent to each other. George and I had raised four children and remembered many times when each of them was "not what we expected." From the very first moment of their arrival, each of our children brought us an ongoing series of surprises. Their unique personalities, behaviors, and needs had regularly stretched us to look beyond our own needs and desires. As they grew older and more independent, their ideas, perspectives, and choices did not necessarily match ours. Listening to and observing our adult children had broadened our view of the world.

Parenting had stretched us in many ways. At times, the stretching process had been easy, even joyful. And at times it had been difficult or painful. Yet George and I were clearly aware that the unexpected surprises of parenting were often precious gifts. Our children had taught us important life lessons, and our lives were far richer and our hearts much bigger because of them.

Expectations of Life

Our daughter's words on meeting her son struck a chord in me. The phrase "this is not what I expected" kept coming back to me over and over in the following months. I began to recognize how clearly the phrase resonated with my overall experience of life. The words "this is not what I expected" echoed like a chime that had been sounding throughout my life. Sometimes the chime had been quiet and almost unnoticed. At other times, the chime had struck in a jarring and unmistakable fashion and knocked me off my feet. The words captured an awareness that was part of my life experience , but which I had never previously grasped so clearly. This was the stark awareness that my entire life was a series of unexpected events.

In the months following our visit to China, I began to look more closely at the many ways in which my life "is not what I expected." I examined my relationship with myself, my relationships with people I am close to and with people in general. I looked at my relationships with a variety of institutions that have been important in my life. And I looked at my relationship with the God in whom I believe. The growing awareness of how much of my life is "not what I expected," how often the people and institutions in my life are "not what I expected," and how even God is "not what I expected" has been valuable for me. It is helping to shape some new attitudes and behaviors. I am able to view my life and the lives of others with increased peace and understanding. I am less demanding of myself and others. I am also comfortable with the realization that the surprises are not over, and that the rest of my life will continue to unfold through the unexpected!

I Am Not What I Expected

I was born at the very start of the baby boom, and I grew up with high ideals and high expectations of myself. I was bright, independent, and hard working— traits that were common in my family. I heard messages like "you can do anything you want" and "you'll go a long way." The words "for of those to whom much is given, much is required" (a John F. Kennedy quote originating in the bible) made a big impact on me. I felt that I was supposed to do something significant, to lead an extraordinary life. I bought into these expectations and spent a good deal of time as an over-achiever. Nonetheless, I was not very sure what I myself wanted from life.

Despite my high ideals, good education, and a strong work ethic, I have not accomplished anything extraordinary in my life. My achievements are modest, and I do not stand out in any of the areas that are usually considered signs of achievement—wealth, prestige or power. I travelled a different path than the one I felt called to in my youth. This occurred in part by following my desires and in part by simply living the life that has been given to me.

Many of the unexpected events of my life journey, events that seemed like speed bumps, detours, roadblocks or dead ends when they occurred, have turned out to be the North Stars of my life. Many of the unexpected happenings on my life road became the navigational tools that helped me travel the journey of my true life. The awareness that unexpected and frequently unwanted events have served as positive guides in my life is one that has unfolded over many years and is still unfolding. The nagging doubt that I have not lived up to my potential (a frequent companion of my younger years) can still rear its ugly head. However, when I listen quietly to the depths of my heart, I realize that my goal has changed from doing something extraordinary to becoming the authentic me. I am also learning that becoming me is a slow process. It is a quiet process. And it frequently involves things that are not what I expected.

My Life Is Not What I Expected

I believe that each of our lives is filled with unexpected events and surprises. I will briefly share four surprises that I feel have greatly affected the journey of my life, events that at the time came totally out of the blue and turned my world upside down to varying degrees. Each surprise was like losing the carefully mapped out plan of my journey, and each surprise eventually became a North Star of my life. I invite you to search through your own life's journey for surprises that have become North Stars.

A major surprise early in my marriage was a move to Nebraska, a state with a broad horizon and vast fields of tall corn. This was a huge change from the landscape of my childhood, and I thought I had moved to the end of the earth. I had grown up in western Washington, among evergreen forests with tall firs, cedars, and hemlocks, interspersed with lush undergrowth. I lived just a few hours from snow covered mountains, rugged ocean beaches, and myriad waterways, islands, and peninsulas. I loved the Northwest, and Nebraska felt very barren and unfamiliar at first.

George and I knew no one when we moved to Lincoln, Nebraska. We had two small children and one short weekend in which to find a home. We chose a small house on a street that was lined with large ash trees and where most of the houses had at least one Big Wheel in the yard. Somehow we managed to hit the jackpot. This was the neighborhood where we raised our family, a neighborhood where children were treasured, where folks looked after each other, where the entire street gathered at the end of each summer for a block party. We made wonderful friends in this neighborhood and the community.

Living in Nebraska provided opportunities I had not expected. Living far from family and old friends gave me a kind of freedom to be who I wanted to be. Distance from family also meant that George and I had to rely on each other. It brought us closer to each other and helped us create the life we wanted for our family. Living in an unfamiliar part of the country taught me that there are many beautiful places to live and that good friends with big hearts can be found everywhere. Life in Nebraska was not the life I had expected, but it was a very good life.

Not long after the surprise of moving to the home of the Cornhuskers, another unexpected event jostled our belief that we were in charge of our lives. We had two children, ages 5 and 3, and decided that we had the love and resources to invite another child into our lives. My first two pregnancies had been smooth and uneventful. I had worked part-time right up to delivery, and we had happy, healthy children. This third pregnancy was not so smooth. I was tired, big, and uncomfortable. Things just didn't seem right. My doctor, who was new to me, suggested this was merely due to the fact that I was older and this was my third pregnancy—not the kind of comments I appreciated. Then, less than two months from my due date, I was visiting an older doctor in the clinic, and he seemed to be taking a long time feeling for the position of the baby. I commented on how active the baby was with lots of pokes from little hands and feet. The doctor's response was that I was feeling so many poking hands and feet because there were two heads. He quickly clarified that I was not carrying a two-headed baby but two separate babies. In shock, I called George from the doctor's office and my announcement met with dead silence on the other end of the line.

"Say something supportive," I pleaded.

After a pause, he said "We'll be just fine, this is wonderful!" And as is the case more often than I like to admit, George was right.

These first two examples of the unexpected in my life occurred in part by my own choice and, though surprising, each of them had positive aspects that were easy to see. The other two examples of unexpected experiences hit me out of the blue, and each of them seemed about as positive as being slammed in the gut by a two-by-four.

The first two-by-four hit a number of years after the birth of our twins and many surprises later. I had just turned 50 and was spending time at the gym, trying to keep myself in shape. I developed a pain in my right shoulder and finally decided to visit an orthopedic physician. During the exam, I mentioned to the physician that I had noticed a slight tremor in my right arm that occurred occasionally in situations that required careful attention. The physician prescribed physical therapy and over the next two months my shoulder improved, although my pride was a bit wounded as I realized that I now resided in a 50-year-old body.

The orthopedic physician had scheduled me for a follow-up visit and during that visit asked me if I was still experiencing the tremor. I said yes and was surprised at the recommendation that I see a neurologist. I am an optimistic person by nature and figured I had a pinched nerve or some simple issue that could be resolved easily and quickly. However, my visit to a local neurologist resulted in an MRI and a variety of tests, but no diagnosis.

143

Next, I was scheduled for a spinal tap; by this point I was getting concerned. When the doctor's office called on the day of my appointment and wanted to reschedule because the doctor was busy that day, my patience reached its limit. I declined the spinal tap and requested a referral to another neurologist at the medical school in Omaha. More tests were performed, and when I was finally diagnosed with Parkinson's Disease, I was horrified. The doctor thought I was overreacting. My symptoms were mild and I was fortunate that it was not a brain tumor or ALS (Lou Gehrig's Disease). Parkinson's is not fatal, he reasoned, and many people live a long time with this chronic, degenerative, incurable, neurological disease.

I wanted to scream at what I saw as the neurologist's insensitivity. I did not feel fortunate. I felt devastated, angry, and frightened. This diagnosis did not fit at all with my image of myself. Parkinson's was a disease of the elderly. Denial worked for a little while, but as I gathered all the information that I could on Parkinson's, it became clear to me that the symptoms being described hit home rather squarely. I experienced all the stages of grief, but was not ready for acceptance. Instead, I responded with an "I'm in charge of my life" attitude.

I fought back with determination, kept physically active, and renewed my dedication to the yoga practice that I had begun a few months previously. My symptoms were managed fairly well with medications, and I reluctantly adjusted to the need for a variety of medications taken several times a day. I did not cut back on my activities, and I continued to work full-time for another ten years, taking on a variety of new challenges. Fatigue was catching up with me however, and eventually, acceptance became more a requirement than an option. I decided to retire with reduced benefits at age 60. I did not have the energy to continue working up to the standards I set for myself.

The second two by four event struck about two years after my retirement in the midst of distractions that decreased its impact for a while. George was retiring, and we were preparing to move to Oregon, where the milder climate would help me maintain physical activity and the natural beauty of the area would nourish my sprit. Everything was in place for the move, but we were in a flurry of activity—last minute packing, closing on the sale of one house and the purchase of another, attending events recognizing George's retirement, a gathering of the many friends we were leaving. In the midst of all this activity, we again experienced the sequence of simple symptoms which led to tests and then to a diagnosis. This time the sequence moved quickly and the diagnosis was non-Hodgkin's lymphoma. We had planned to spend our final days in Nebraska in Omaha with our son and daughter-in-law and our two small grandchildren. These days kept me afloat. They reminded me of all I had to live for and let me live in the joy of the present moment.

As we drove away from Omaha and headed west to Oregon, George and I were calm, but concerned. Twelve years had passed since my Parkinson's diagnosis. We both had become students in the school of dealing with the unexpected and living in the present. Were we ready for a hands-on opportunity to learn about mortality?

My initial response to this opportunity was "thanks, but no thanks." I regressed back to my familiar "can-do" attitude. My sister connected me with an outstanding lymphoma specialist, and we chose the most aggressive level of treatment that my body could handle. I shaved my head before my hair had a chance to fall out, we travelled to Disneyworld with our son and his family between aggressive chemotherapy treatments. Internally, I was confused and frightened, but my external message was "I can handle this." Then, following the next-to-last scheduled chemotherapy treatment, I developed a bronchial infection that knocked me flat, and I knew it was time to face reality and slow down.

Others Are Not What I Expected

Everyone reading this book has certainly experienced situations or times where others have not met their expectations. The others can be individuals we know well, such as family members, friends, or colleagues. We have expectations of those who produce, transport, sell and repair the goods we need in our everyday lives. We have expectations of people who help us maintain our physical, mental, and spiritual well-being—physicians and other medical personnel, teachers and coaches, ministers, priests, rabbis. We have expectations of civic and world leaders. The list goes on and on. Chances are, most readers could come up with a lengthy list of times when their expectations of others were not met. In addition to individuals who do not meet our expectations, we all have experience with institutions that are not what we expected—governments, the military, financial institutions, academic institutions, hospitals and clinics, employers, even our churches.

As I have reflected on the people in my life who were not what I expected I have learned a lot about myself and become more aware of the expectations I set for others. When I am able to temper my expectations of another, it removes a great burden from both of us. It teaches me to view others with the kind of compassion and forgiveness I would hope to receive from people whose expectations I have not met.

God is Not What I Expected

A few months after our trip to China, I was struck by a gospel reading whose words seemed to parallel what our daughter had said when she met her son. The words almost jumped off the page as I read a familiar Advent scripture passage in which John the Baptist sends a messenger to Jesus. Through the messenger, John asks Jesus "Are you the one who is to come, or should we look for another?" The words stayed with me and stewed for a time, and I knew they had a message for me. I began to understand that I had essentially asked this question of God many times in my life. As I had moved from a childlike relationship with God to a more mature, adult relationship, I had frequently found that God "was not what I expected." In addition, I realized that my response to God was not what I expected nor was the response of many others. I was also acutely aware that despite my lifelong connection to and love for the Catholic Church, the institutional church very often was "not what I expected".

How often have I felt that God "was not what I expected"? How often have I wanted to "look for another," a God whose world was perfect, without suffering and death? Jesus' response to the messenger of John the Baptist is also a response to me. "Go and tell John what you hear and see; the blind regain their sight, the lame walk, lepers are cleansed, the deaf hear, the dead are raised and the poor have the good news proclaimed to them. And blessed is the one who takes no offense at me." As this passage has taken root in my soul, I have gradually become aware that this "unexpected" God is indeed my God. And for that I am grateful.

My God is a God of surprises. How about your God? Some of us expect a God of power and might who "has the whole world in his hands" and keeps everything running smoothly. Surprise! God gave us free will and put the world also in our hands. We may expect a God who rules over us with authority, who rewards and punishes us according to our merits. Surprise! God sends Jesus who tells about our unfathomable God through stories—the parable of the Prodigal Son, the story of the shepherd who leaves the 99 sheep to find the one sheep who is lost. Jesus tells us that we are to forgive another 70 times seven, in other words, without limit. We may expect a God whose glory and majesty overwhelms us. Surprise! The unfathomable God becomes incarnate. A young unmarried girl of deep faith accepts God's invitation to the unexpected. Jesus is born into poverty, grows up quietly, lives a simple life ministering to the poor and the outcasts. He welcomes common people, sinners, women, foreigners. Finally he is betrayed, ridiculed, humiliated and led to die a public and agonizing death.

My God is indeed a God of surprises. God is not always what I expect. God is much, much more.

Living in Expectation

The growing awareness that life is "not what I expected" has been a surprisingly freeing experience. It is helping me learn to live life more graciously. Knowing that life is full of the unexpected has led me to a better acceptance of myself and of others. It has diminished my desire to try to control events in my life or the lives of others. I spent much of my life driven by an anxious need to accomplish things. I was always in a rush, moving quickly from one thing to another or multi-tasking several projects at once. I expected good results from everything I did, and I rarely took time to appreciate or enjoy the results. I had more things to do.

I also frequently expected similar speed, efficiency, and outstanding results from others. I am sure that the expectations I set for my spouse, my children, my extended family, my friends and my colleagues were at times unrealistic and oppressive.

Awareness that life and that God are full of the unexpected has allowed me to better accept others and myself as we are. I am better able to live in the now, and I have less need to try to control events in my life or the lives of others. I am slowly learning to live my life at a calmer pace. I am learning to wait and to listen.

My God is a God of surprises. I live in expectation of the unexpected. When I internalize these beliefs, my life changes. Desire for what I do not have is replaced by gratitude for what I do have. The need for control of others and myself is replaced with compassion and forgiveness for others and myself. The desire to do well and be well thought of is replaced by openness to become my true self.

My God, as you walk with me
Calm my restless and willful spirit
Teach me your ways
To walk with a spirit of kindness
To recognize your abundant gifts
To give and forgive each day
To listen quietly for your voice
To wait with patience
To live with gratitude always

Closer Than Our Own Skin

by Beth Patterson

MY GRANDMOTHER VERNA died in 2001 at the age of 103 with her boots on, as the saying goes. Her body was broken down by the years, but her mind and spirit remained strong to the very end.

Gram was born in 1898 to two itinerant Methodist minister "circuit riders." She was the oldest of five children. From that generation, especially as the oldest child of strict upbringing, she took on the values of absolute and unthinking service to her family and others as a sacred trust. By the time I came along in the 1950's she was herself in her 50's, trying to put together a new life and recovering from an extremely abusive marriage, the death of one of her sons during World War II, severe mental illness in her other son, and the sense that the "picture" that she had painted about what her life was supposed to look like was blurred and distorted.

By the time my mother, her oldest of two daughters, died in the late 1970's of ovarian cancer, Gram's picture of how life works had been completely turned upside down. Possibly because of the trauma of her lifetime, her faith in the God of her fathers was strong, but not necessarily flexible. Gram had come to view life as something to be survived rather than cherished as unpredictable, unknowable and wild. Gram's life had been full of great sorrow and very little adventure, although she had wonderful life-long friends, and grand-, great-grand- and great-great-grandchildren who adored her.

While my relationship with Gram was one of the most solid and grounded in my life, there were some things we didn't talk about. One of them was my liberal stance on politics and spirituality. Although I knew that I stood on my mother's shoulders, and she on Gram's, the gulf was too wide for us to dialogue around certain key life issues. Gram wanted to be able to understand my less constructed spirituality, but we did not have the same framework. We would occasionally talk about the issues but could never directly address them, as the potential for rift between us was something neither of us wanted to risk.

In 1992 as I was in seminary in Colorado, Gram was living in an assisted living community in central Florida. She was 94 and going strong. One day she fell and broke her hip, or her hip broke and she fell. She hit her head in the fall and wasn't able to use the electronic "lifeline." She wasn't found in her little apartment until several hours later, and though rushed to the emergency room, she nearly died. Strapped to a gurney, Gram had a near-death experience, which she related to me a few months later while I was visiting her in Florida. At first I was dismayed that she hadn't told me about the experience on the phone, but I came to realize that this was such a powerful turning point for her that it could only be transmitted face to face.

In the near-death experience, Gram was in a long rectangular "room" with curtains drawn in front and behind her. The curtains were of no particular color, nor were they white. They were not opaque; they seemed translucent. She said that the setting reminded her of a train or bus station. Somehow she knew that the curtain behind her clearly signified separation from her life up to that time; the curtain in front symbolized her continued existence after physical death. A wall was on her right, but she could recall no wall on her left. As she took all of this in, she felt a Presence sitting close to her on her left. When I pressed her for clarity she hesitantly called the entity Jesus. I'm quite sure the hesitancy came from humility, not lack of clarity. She never turned her head to look at him.

They had a long wordless conversation about what being in that particular moment in her life meant. Gram was emphatic about the fact that they didn't talk with words. Rather they communicated mind to mind, heart to heart. She recalled feeling like there was no past or future. They talked about whether she should choose to return to life on this side of the curtain (the side before physical death) or go forward. Up to that point, she didn't know that she had a choice. The surprise in her voice as she told me about this was endearing and gave me a catch in my throat.

They talked about an incident for which she had not forgiven herself for more than 40 years. In our late night chats when I visited her prior to this event, she would allude to this sin for which she could not forgive herself. I never knew exactly what it was but had my guesses.

In this experience, Jesus said to her, "Verna, I know you've asked for forgiveness for something time and again, but for the Life of me, I can't remember what it is."

In recalling this moment Gram said, "And you know, I can't seem to remember it now either." Gram had an incredible memory so I don't think she meant this literally. I think through this encounter she had allowed her memory be wiped clean of judgment and rhetoric.

In describing the entire experience, there was much detail and much that lacked words, but tears and body language spoke of the immensity of experience.

Part of the conversation with Jesus was about how to "be" if she decided to return to this side, the pre-physical-death side of the curtain. He suggested that she just continue to talk to him like she was doing at that moment—all the time. When she expressed misgivings about how she could do so, he just gently recommended that she try it and see how it worked. When she asked if it would be better for her family for her to stay where she was, on that side, he suggested that she might be just as useful on this, the pre-death side of the curtain. This non-linearity was an astounding idea for pragmatic Gram.

Gram said that she felt fully awake during this encounter, and that coming back to this side she started to fall back asleep. She said she knew she would wake up again when she actually did go to the other side of that curtain, and she seemed to be much less fearful of dying after this revelation.

When she tried to tell me about her experience of Jesus, she was wordless. She just said how surprisingly close he was. I stumblingly paraphrased a Biblical phase "Gram, is he closer than a brother?"

"No, Beth," she replied quickly and firmly. "He is closer than your own skin."

I remember taking in my breath sharply, as I felt my understanding of ancestral wisdom take a quantum leap. Somehow I knew that her words would be a Lighthouse for the rest of my life—to understand and experience spiritual lineage in a cellular Light.

After this experience, Gram's personal and spiritual boundaries expanded immensely. She was much freer to express her feelings of love and yet more detached from the result. She was alternately disturbed, amused and delighted by the way life opened before her. She had always had a grounded spiritual presence, now she moved to a new level of understanding of the human condition and her own place in the world.

She was able to describe—without using the specific word—*detachment*. She was now able to see her role as matriarch with more perspective. She found herself interested in other spiritual paths, other ways of living in the world. She and I could now talk of my spiritual journey and share things that I wouldn't have imagined being able to share earlier in our relationship.

On her 99th birthday, I asked her as I did every year, "What did you learn this year, Gram?"

She responded without hesitation, "I had to re-think my theology again this year. I always thought that it was my job to worry and try to keep all of you [her extended family] on the straight and narrow path to heaven. Now I know that all I have to do is love you. That's **all** I have to do!"

Gram's new-found amazement with life's mystery stayed with her until her death at 103. She slipped a little here and there into worry and fretting over her family but, by and large, she was free.

Gram's transformation into freedom from the known is the template for my life. While I have started my adult life with an expanded picture of the mystery, thanks in large part to my Grandmother's and Mother's love, I know that my life's work is to continuously be transforming from what is known to what is unknown. For this I am grateful and cranky, hopeful and anxious.

As I work to eliminate my anxiety about my own family's well being, Gram's words on her 99th birthday bounce around inside my head, "You just have to love them, Beth, that's all you have to do!" What has ceased to be remarkable about this is that I feel her "just loving me" from wherever she is, and her love and guidance are instantly available anytime I ask for them.

Gram comes to me in many ways; her presence is most clear when my mind wants to attach to something and name it, label it, quantify it. I feel her gentle spirit saying, "Not this. Not that, Beth. Keep on seeing more clearly."

And so in this tenth year of the anniversary of her death, I affirm her life within me. She is closer than my skin. She is in the breath that I breathe, the thoughts that I think. She literally is my inspiration. *Thank you and deep bows of gratitude to you, dear Gram, for your spiritual mentoring. It continues past your physical death, just as Jesus said it would.*

And what's more, Gram and all of our ancestors are available for each of us. Ancestors become a communal, as well as personal, pool of wisdom, guidance and inspiration. While we are closer to the spiritual and familial ancestral lineage, the field of available love for us to draw on is unlimited and abundant.

There's no lack of anything in this universe. It's all closer than our skin. It just takes being willing to tune our receivers to a different frequency—and let go of our preconceived ideas of what it's all about, to open constantly to what is not yet known.

One Day at a Time

by Gayle Yamasaki

I HAVE BEEN journaling since I was 18 years old. These are excerpts from my journal during a difficult soul-searching, self-searching time.

February 8, 2009

I am determined to save the only life I could save!

I was told last Friday (1/30/09) that my contract at the college would not be renewed. In six months my current contractual obligations will be over. On that telling day, I will have spent 15 years and two months of my life work at this institution. The longest work commitment I have made to date to any one "employer." I have been relinquished of my role as director and now banished/assigned to "special projects" which I can perform at home.

I need to reach out to my sangha (community), my anam cara (soul friends). I would invite them to hold me in their thoughts and prayers as I make this journey. I want to ask them to help me create a space of being together, a communal space around me where I can distinguish my inner voice of truth from the inner voice of fear. I ask that they bear witness to my self-discovery sharpening my sense of self and strengthening my resolve to follow my inner teacher.

I also relentlessly turn to books that have provided me solace in the past, those bits and pieces of wisdom, scattered and swirl around me like confetti. I try to grab hold of pieces, my life is swirling. These pieces reflect my life story, where will they land? What new whole will be created?

I know this is a significant passage for me; although I have no idea how long this voyage will be. I trust that there is still work and contribution for me to do. I have yet to imagine its form and shape. Is this a universal longing, having something yet to do in this world? I confess that it is in the darkness of the night and in the early morning before dawn that questions haunt me:

What will grow out of this experience?

How will it change my life?

What purpose might it serve?

At 55 I recognize this as a turning point. I can no longer return to what was before. I know that I am experiencing the loss of my "job" personally, and that I am a part of a collective community of Americans, hundreds of thousands. I am not alone. I am now connected to others and to the suffering that only compassionate acts can alleviate. This loss of my job is an initiation into the *fellowship* of those who bear the mark of pain. It feels as if the suffering of thousands has crossed a threshold, and it is overturning the order of the soul. I am hopeful that by catching sight of the Buddha nature in all, I can survive this without losing my hope or my way. When I can catch sight of the goodness, perhaps I can do well in a wounded world—by being the storycatcher. Am I being called back to my "hidden wholeness" my "Buddha nature" as life stories swirl around me?

Sometimes life comes along again and tests us on the principles we stand for and our teaching. It's as if life says, "Let's see if you really mean what you say. Can you bring action to the teachings?" Is this my karma, an ordeal of suffering in which my beliefs and relationships are tested? I know that there will be mourning and grief for what I have lost.

Yet I intuitively know I have been freed from a setting that was steadily killing off my spirit. Freed from an obligation that I have not been courageous enough to make myself. Will I dare to take my heart in my hands and walk through an invisible wall into a new life, (didn't Harry Potter do that)?

February 20, 2009

What is beyond what I have valued in the past?
Where am I being called, being drawn?
How will I choose to live out that calling?
How do I honor the desire?
How do I listen and follow the energy?

I have spent the past two weeks preparing to present my life work on paper—responding to the call for a resume, a list of my work experiences, where have I been till today? What have I been called, where have I bid that calling, whom have I served, and what good did I contribute? The events in our lives happen in a sequence in time, but their significance to us . . .They find their own order.

How we remember, and what we remember and why we remember, form the most personal map of our individuality. I have to become willing to REMEMBER.

The episodic way in which our lives evolve: childhood, adolescence, college, career, marriage, divorce, illness, motherhood—life as a single mother, life without our mother's, at each stage we have both laughter and tears. We have lived many lives and each one has left an indelible mark.

As I jolted memory to visit me, I record the dates of my work experiences. How do I share all that I've learned through a "job title?" I must tempt and seduce with words the "other's" interest—enough to have the "other" curious, yet grounded in confidence that somehow where I have been and what I have done will instill assurance that I have what it takes to perform this task they need in this job title they have prescribed for the work needing to be done.

There are serendipitous events that connect experience to opportunity. I have stood often in that threshold of "no longer and not yet." Wondering what direction to paddle, approaching the river's divide, taking the one I hoped less traveled. It has always made all the difference. Yet difference seems to be analyzed only in hindsight as we remember why we chose that way; but perhaps it was that the way chose us.

Yet those job titles and time spent in a place also forces me to recall painful and joyous memories. If I had not fled my marriage and my dissertation to Rock Springs, I would not have met women who in these 25 years form the foundation of my circle of trust. I would not have had Alysia. Had I not fled from Rock Springs to Klamath Falls because my job title had become too constricting with unreasonable demands to produce revenue with non-existent products and capabilities, I would not have learned how spiritually strong I was through Alysia's disease. Perhaps she would not have gotten ill if we had not come to Klamath Falls. Here I found spiritual direction, finding a space where what I intuitively trusted now had a place and language to call home. Because my original job title was eliminated, Martha Anne created and challenged me to a new calling of working to provide opportunities and hope for youth. I would not have met Jeff, I would not have known that I have gifts as a "story catcher," that perhaps my initial calling of counselor is part of my destiny.

All these remembrances reveal glimmers of our true selves at that moment in time yet collectively contribute to who we are today. Each memory comes bearing a gift for us if we look for it—a peace offering—that there is nothing to fear in our pasts. They only ask to be remembered.

What do I bring forth to my next work after 55 years, soon 56 on March 4? Only now am I sensing that I am to embark on what I am called to BE in this second half of my life. I am in that liminal space in the threshold. How do I trust where I am being drawn? It is too easy to be seduced by false security. Yet I know that there are realities of needs in this world for me: health insurance for Alysia.

As I search and desire to move towards that which is life giving, I also acknowledge my own expectations and disappointments. They too will be a part of my remembrances and yes they too provide Peace offerings.

June 17, 2009

As I sink into my final month of "employment" at the college, I am grateful for these past five months. You probably wonder what has she been doing? What has she been feeling? What will she do? These are all worthy questions I would think given the situation that I am in.

So here is a brief summary of my doings, I have:

Sharpened my resume; after all I haven't really seriously looked for a job in over a decade.

Talked with an attorney.

Talked with a financial advisor.

Attended not one but two retirement workshops.

Talked with human resources about the details of closing my accounts.

Applied for jobs.

Had several interviews. Rejected by some, silence from others.

Created a home office. Several years ago I made the decision to do work only at work so I converted the home office into a guest bedroom, took the computer out and turned off the Internet.

Created an office downtown with an official mailing address and workstation.

I have felt relief, gratitude, sadness, anger, betrayed, and unappreciated. That shared; there has not been one day since I walked off the campus that I had a longing for my job there. I have gone to the Shasta Abbey (a Buddhist temple and retreat center). It has helped me re-center and become more faithful to my tradition, more faithful to myself.

I have kayaked at 5:30 in the morning and under the full moon. I have witnessed the birthing of Canadian goslings and mallard ducklings. I have shared breakfast with bald eagles, osprey, grebes, white pelicans, turtles, minks, and river otters. I have snow shoed at Crater Lake in spring snow with no one there but the silence, a needed respite.

I went to Spain and spent Mother's Day and Alysia's 21st birthday there. I am living a simpler life and know what it means to be in community. I have honored and celebrated friends who have died and witnessed the beginning of new life with children I have known for years as they walk across their graduation stage to a life that is waiting for them.

Perhaps the best of what I am is now being called upon. To really listen for the work that is calling me.

I have read countless books on how to live from Suze Orman, Mary Oliver, Parker Palmer, Carolyn Myss, and Sarah Lawrence Lightfoot's *Third Chapter*, anything that catches my imagination.

What I do now is what I know is important to my day. No more reading countless e-mails and feeling a need to respond timely to everyone . . . so much for building social capital. I am quieting my wants and recognizing my needs.

I am grateful to my spiritual director, my anam cara group of wise women (we meet every other month, have for the past, now, four years). Swimming and water aerobics continue to contribute to my health, as well as walking for transportation and biking (last year's tax incentive expenditure). I have gone to a naturopath and received acupuncture for the first time, recommitted to a healthier diet. Yes, I have made a lot of money over my lifetime, and I have had the opportunity to now pause and wonder: where did it go?

But that was my past, and today is my present. I anticipate filing for unemployment July 1 (joining million of Americans and grateful for this safety net), paying out of pocket for health insurance (which I am grateful to be able to afford for myself and Alysia), living simply, but with heartfelt abundance (which feeling I hope will last), and moving deeper into my spiritual practice and life work.

I thank those who have remained a constant in my life. I am grateful for the phone calls, e-mails, prayers, cards, letters, and gifts all. I wish all of us well and hope for the best. Sh'ma,

September 12, 2009

I am thinking about accomplishments today.

Is what I have accomplished in my life truly what I love?

How do I measure my accomplishments?

What measuring devise do I use?

For I am an ordinary being who has experienced and witnessed extraordinary wonders.

In hindsight, working backwards, do I realize that some of the things I am most proud of have not necessarily been times of joy and happiness but those that took an inner courage that I did not know I had? I withstood and moved through those life-changing events and found light on the threshold, on the other side.

I have felt deep loneliness or perhaps it was such a deep wanting of love that I wore my loneliness, clear to others, yet I did not know how transparent my longing was. I found envy and jealously. I think today, I'd call those moments a dissatisfaction and discomfort of my own skin.

But I suspect those experiences have allowed me emotionally and psychologically to enter many lives— like closed doors to be opened not knowing what I'll find. But in those times I also found myself discovering and accepting SPIRT in my life. An accomplishment?

I had to be five years old. I remember climbing a banyan tree across the street from my house. This was huge tree. It had dangling pieces of root that looked like monkeys' tails. I held on to one tail, swinging and swaying, feeling myself moving with the wind. My sturdy legs wrapped around that monkey's tail. I was the wind. I hung on. The wind and that root held me and I became one with the sway. Enthralled, enraptured, ecstatic, I was one with this tail. My mind wiped clear of explanation, existing in a pure state of relationship, a beyond-word experience. An accomplishment?

I want to open myself up to the stillness. It has taken decades, for my mind was not trained for stillness. My mind has been most occupied by a highly opinionated, contentious committee of stimulating and persistent characters. I have stood before my bathroom mirror and seen one face looking back at me, but inside is the joyous child, the overbearing critic, the optimist, the doubter, the judge and the jury. It has taken many lifetimes to sort through enough of these voices to have an even chance to serve as a moderator of my inner committees. An accomplishment?

In the decade of my 20's, I spent significant time and money learning psychotherapy, assisting others to access their autonomy, to become their own self and to master their fates. Perhaps I was looking for my own peace of mind. I know now that no amount of therapeutic intervention, however, provides peace of mind. An accomplishment?

I have had other beyond word experiences. The birth of my daughter Alysia. Being a single mother/head of household, finding a village to raise my child. Traveling at 18 for three months in America, camping and hiking in our National Parks, stunned at the wonders of our natural world. Discovering the underwater sea world, the freedom of movement side by side with giant sea turtles. Standing in the midst of giant redwoods, the scent of the earth. The miracle of having another's kidney give life to Alysia, one life ends but allows another to live. An accomplishment?

Mixing certainty of purpose with surrender to surprise. How to live a life of openness, entering an unimagined life? Perhaps its like that five-year-old girl holding on to that monkey's tail, being the wind, enthralled, enraptured, ecstatic. An accomplishment?

December 1, 2009

Welcome 2010.

I realize that the life I am living is not the same as the life that wants to live in me. It is so difficult to "let go" of the familiar, the routine, the proven, the daily rituals; so hard to relinquish the solidity, the expertise, the status and station and take the risk of embracing the new, the unproven, and unfamiliar. It has been a time of fear, ambivalence, chaos during which it has been hard to articulate where I am or where I am heading or how I will get there.

I find myself in between stories. The old one is gone and the new one is just beginning to take shape.

Who am I now that I am not employed in academia, higher education? Who am I now that my days are not dictated by the demands and challenges of an institution? I find in this time of change that all the things that I took to be me, all the roles and responsibilities and reactions and conditions I identified as my self, reveal no self at all.

This in between times, I admit. I have found it difficult to simply stay with no story and no self. There is this emptiness at the center. This gap in my story allows me to see how I am not what I do, allows me to create and play within new stories, new roles, without identifying exclusively with them.

Freed from identifying with the story of the life I was living at the College and not identified with any story of my life in this new place, I experience all the movements as "story catching." But these wanderings have brought me back to a place that is familiar, a place of silence and listening, a place of story.

What will be in my storybook? I came into this life as a blank book, pages waiting to fill. It may not be what literally happened to me, but what I make out of what happened to me. What I share with others is what I remember. It is also how I will be remembered. My storybook reflects what I did with the time given me. The time between the blank page, the day I was born and the final chapter, the closing of the book the day I die.

So in 2010 I want to invite others to share with me a story. They say that a picture is worth a thousand words, but we can't get the whole picture unless we have the whole story. And the magic in words is that the story can make the picture. What is the story you are tending, the one you will never let be put out?

Tell me that story.

This will be my invitation in 2010. For I believe that all our remembrances reveal glimmers of our true selves at that moment in time. And collectively contribute to who we are today. What if each memory comes bearing a gift for us, like those pieces of confetti floating and swirling in the air around us, all PEACE offerings. There is nothing to fear; our pasts only ask to be remembered.

With this invitation I want to welcome others to join with me in creating an interpersonal community space in which we can hold story with each other. Together we can create a community of listening. This can be a place to turn, a sacred space where we place our peace offerings to each other and the world. We can hold our hearts like a talking piece in our hands. Inviting each other to tell that story. The one we will never let be put out.

Let us enter 2010 with new clarity that the gift of life is ours only for a while. Let us live into that choice. Let us see with new clarity that all the life around us is something precious to the earth. May we find more and more ways to honor this in all sentient beings and ourselves.

June 26, 2011

What a long time it can take to become the person one has always been.

I believe that we all have a longing to be remembered. It is through honoring our personal experiences through story, that we can be remembered. I have sat with many people over these past months listening for story. My practice for meaning-making now is one of a story catcher. What is that story that you have been tending? What is your

story that can never be put out? I invite you to tell me that story at: storycatcherathome@gmail.com
    In gassho, Gayle.

Dancing Through the Storm

by Charlotte Bloebaum

Life isn't about waiting for the storm to pass, it's about learning how to dance in the rain. -- anonymous

MY FAITH LIFE often seems like a dance to me. There are many times I'm off on my own, separate, like a Flamenco dancer giving full expression to my passion for the music, aware of my Partner but not always connected or even in sync. Though I'm always trying to follow the beat, sometimes my rhythm gets off, there is a dissonance in the music, or I lose my place in the steps. Then suddenly the music changes and my Partner reaches out to draw me closer for an embrace and to better lead me in this dance of my life.

As a young woman living in the Midwest, I felt God's strong presence in my life and believed God was waltzing me through the steps I needed to follow. In 1961, at the age of 18, I was baptized into the Roman Catholic Church. I was full of religious zeal and took my faith very seriously—at least for a while—following all Church rules to the letter, believing that was what God wanted for and expected of me.

Over the ensuing years, I began to hear God's voice in different kinds of music and experimented with a variety of other dance moves, exploring other spiritual practices, traditions and religions. I was in and out of the Church for many years—more often out than in. Although my husband Joe and I were married in a Catholic Church, I drifted away until our two children were born. Since I had not been raised in a faith tradition, I felt it was important to provide that for our children, Jane and Chris. I returned to the Catholic Church that had first captured my heart and sent our children to Catholic schools.

In 1981, Joe understood there was a job for him in Portland, Oregon, so he and I, Jane and Chris, a rather large dog, several cats and a couple of hamsters moved from the Midwest to Portland. It was a traumatic experience for all of us. The children had to leave their friends and adjust to a new school. We didn't know anyone in Oregon, and the man who had promised Joe the job was ultimately unable to produce it because the funding did not come through. I found work, Joe was getting unemployment, and we had some money from the sale of our house so we decided to stay and make the best of it. We enrolled our children in the school at the parish we were attending, and they seemed to settle in fairly easily.

Our daughter Jane graduated from eighth grade and went on to a Catholic high school, where she seemed comfortable, at least for awhile.

We planned for our son Chris to graduate from the parish school as well, but the school decided to eliminate their middle school grades, so Chris began seventh grade at public junior high school. This transition seemed to usher in some very challenging times for him and for us. Although he had shown signs of some problems in grade school, his teachers were able to give him individual attention and better monitor his progress because the classes were smaller. His teachers called us if he failed to turn in work or was falling behind, and we were thus able to stay on top of his progress. But public school was a different story.

In those days, very little was known about attention deficit disorder, learning disabilities and other behavioral problems in children, so getting outside help wasn't really a feasible option.

On his first day of classes as a high school freshman, we received a phone call from the school. Chris had skipped class, left campus with friends and been caught smoking marijuana. We were asked to come and get him. This was the beginning of my nightmare.

At first, I felt sorry for him and tried to convince myself that he was just following the crowd. I wanted to believe this was a one-time occurrence and wouldn't happen again. I tried giving him encouragement, support and sympathy, I offered to help with homework—all of the things parents do when they see their children headed down the wrong road. Inside, however, I was angry that he could pull such a dumb stunt and get into trouble on the very first day of high school.

Unfortunately, it wasn't a one-time event; the situation soon got worse—much worse. We began to receive phone calls from the school that he was not turning in his work; he was being disruptive and failing several classes. We talked with Chris to try to find out what the problem was. He told us he was very unhappy. The new school was much larger, he felt lost and all the kids seemed to already know one another. Chris is an artist and while the public school acknowledged that he had artistic ability, it had no program to help the creative process bloom.

We decided to look into an alternative school. The new school conducted an in-depth interview with Chris and with me. We were all relieved when he was accepted, and he began classes that January. The school actually encouraged the creative process and had a pass/fail system. We were thrilled with his progress and for a while, he seemed to do well.

In contrast to Chris' seeming to find his place, I was growing disenchanted with Catholicism and began to pursue my connection to the Divine in other ways. I started exploring other paths, reading about earth-based religions such as Wicca, magic, shamanism. During this time it often felt as if I were dancing alone.

These alternative spiritual paths I pursued seemed to all encourage meditation as an integral part of the practice. I knew nothing about meditation, but it was in the back of my mind one day when I was at Chris' school. I noticed a flyer for an adult education class that taught participants how to meditate. I signed up and started the following week. The meditation teacher spent the first session explaining about meditation and a few different traditions before we actually practiced sitting. It seemed impossible for me to sit still, and I quickly got discouraged. At the end of the session he announced that he would be out of town for the next two weeks for his regular job. He recommended an alternative instructor at another location for that two-week period but gave us the incorrect time for that class.

The next week my group walked into the studio he had directed us to expecting to find a meditation class but finding instead a man instructing a group of adults in what seemed like ridiculous movements and poses. I was not sure what they were doing. When he noticed our arrival, he commented that we must be "Paul's meditation group" and laughed a bit, saying our teacher had given us the wrong time. He explained that the meditation class would not begin for another hour but invited us to join what he called his yoga class.

This "accident" of timing was my introduction to what was to become a life-long love and a valuable practice that would eventually lead me back into the Catholic Church.

We all joined in the class and followed the movements as he coached us. I found I very much enjoyed the non-threatening and completely non-competitive discipline of yoga. As a younger woman, I had been a dance instructor, and this movement class felt like heaven. But it was nothing like the rigid ballet discipline I had done for many years. Some of our group came early again the following week for the yoga class, and after our two weeks ended, we inquired about continuing the yoga classes. The instructor said he was substituting for the regular teacher who owned the studio but was on vacation. He assured us we would be welcome to drop in for one of her classes any time. Although the class had continued to stick in my mind as something I knew would be good for me, it was not until a year or so later that I felt pulled back into the embrace of my Partner and was led back to yoga.

I continued with the meditation class and at the end of the six-week course, I felt as if I "got it" but did not put much effort into my own daily practice.

By the middle of that school year Chris had become argumentative, surly, and disruptive, and he insisted he was going to quit school. We refused to sign the necessary papers; he was not yet 17 and needed our permission to drop out. However, he somehow managed to quit on his own, without our approval. He found someone to live with, packed up his things and left. My heart broke.

The summer of 1987, I went on a rafting trip with friends and realized what bad shape I was in. Cigarette smoking for many years had left me short of breath, and I was overweight, flabby and soft, and had no energy. The following week I screwed up my courage and walked into the yoga class. The regular instructor was an amazing woman. She seemed to be able to move her body in any direction and stretch it to unlimited places. I was fascinated and wanted to be able to move that way myself. I attended every week, sitting in the back so no one would notice me, and went home each week feeling much better.

At the end of each session, we had a rest period—Shavasana it is called in yogic terms. During this time our instructor would read out of a spiritual book, which surprised me. What did spirituality have to do with physical discipline, I wondered. But my mind was captivated and I began to read more about yoga. I soon realized yoga means union—union of body, mind, and spirit. This was a very different concept for me: the physical body actually affects one's soul and mental abilities.

My inquiry and study continued; I became a vegetarian and within a year had a very different body and outlook. The yoga instructor taught us breathing exercises that cleared our minds and our bodies. Not long after I started attending her classes every day after work I was able to stop smoking. When she mentioned she was leading a meditation group on Monday evenings, I began to stay and sit with that group.

She taught us mental exercises that helped our focus and led us into true centering meditation. During these sessions she often mentioned various spiritual teachers including Buddha, Jesus, and various Indian swamis who had come to the U.S. to teach. She also mentioned her own spiritual teacher. Curious, I asked her more about him because he was also from the Midwest, although he had passed away a year or so earlier. She loaned me some tapes of his lectures, and I discovered his talks often centered on

Jesus and the Divine Mother and how they are always with us. Again, I was fascinated by this connection.

During this period, I accompanied my yoga/meditation teacher on retreats and continued to attend her meditation classes for many years. I decided to train to become a Yoga teacher myself and this deepening of my studies of Yoga helped me fully realize how closely our bodies, minds and spirits work together to make us whole and complete humans. As one of my teachers shared: "We are spiritual beings sent to earth to have a human experience."

I was finally beginning to understand and really know what the phrases "God and I are one—I and God are one" and "Let go and let God" meant. In the book *Yoga Sutras of Patanjali*," written many years ago, the author Patanjali stresses the point that yoga is NOT a religion; rather, it is a spiritual practice open to anyone of any religion or with no particular religion or belief; every yoga teacher I have had has confirmed this.

Many who begin the practice of yoga find, as I was beginning to understand, that it strengthens and supports their own faith/spiritual tradition. Eventually, the spirituality and depth of this practice led me to return to the Catholic Church, realizing that in some ways All Gods are One God. There have been several Catholic authors, including Jesuit Father Anthony de Mello, who have written about and taught the benefits of practicing yoga and meditation along with one's faith tradition. The two really do work hand in hand. Through yoga and meditation I felt God taking my hand again and was willing to follow God's lead in what was to become a very challenging and stormy dance.

At the beginning of Chris' junior year, the alternative school changed its curriculum to be more in line with other public schools. Under this new system, many of the teachers who had helped him so much left the school. The final blow came when the counselor with whom he had worked and learned to trust could no longer be his counselor; the school had decided to assign students to counselors based on their last names. Chris was uprooted from a fragile bond of trust because his last name started with the wrong letter of the alphabet! We begged and pleaded to allow him to remain with the original counselor but to no avail. We knew he was feeling lost; what we didn't know was that Chris had begun using drugs on a regular basis.

Embracing the disciplines of yoga and meditation provided me a place of solace and sanity that would help me survive the ensuing nightmare years of dealing with what had become a full-blow drug addiction for Chris. They also made me take a good hard look at myself, my relationship with Joe and begin to understand that we were all responsible for caring for each other.

I realized that our family life was very dysfunctional. I had been in denial about Joe's drinking problem for years. Finally I accepted that we had not set a particularly good example for our children; I blamed myself for Chris's drug problem.

Through my prayer and yoga/meditation practice, eventually I learned to forgive myself. Yoga and meditation never ask us to beat ourselves up but only to take a good hard look at ourselves and our lives to see ways we can improve them. The disciplines discourage guilt feelings and encourage self-improvement. But it took many years for me to learn these very difficult lessons.

About six months after he dropped out of high school and moved out, Chris called and asked to move back home. We allowed him to on condition that he either return to school or get a job. He was determined to not return to school so he found a part-time job.

Where, I often wondered during this time, was this loving God I had believed in and tried to help our children believe in? God surely did not seem to be present in our house during this time.

My feelings were spinning out of control. Joe and I were furious with Chris; we believed he was ruining his life and would never amount to anything. I wanted to lash out at him for being so ridiculous and not listening to us. I felt he didn't really know what he wanted, that Joe and I knew better what would be good for him and his future, and that would be to finish school and prepare for a career. In hindsight I admit I was more interested in punishing him and trying to convince him that we, his parents, were right. I never considered that he was a very troubled young man.

I hadn't yet realized the damage this anger was doing to me and my family. I had become blind and couldn't admit that the approach Joe and I were using to use to try to get Chris' cooperation—or, more truthfully, try to regain control—was, in reality, driving a deeper wedge between us. This frustration led to angry words we later wished we'd never said. Although we never hurt him physically, the arguing, shouting, and dark and chaotic environment we were living in was most certainly abusive to all of us.

It was during these incredibly dark times that my yoga practice was instrumental in regaining control of myself. It helped me understand that I need to live in the here and now, and that I am not responsible for the self-destructive choices others make. I can encourage and support, but in the end, each person must do his or her own work. No God or teacher is going to step in and just "fix everything." Although I could accept God might not fix this problem, I often found myself very angry with God. It felt as if my Dance Partner was intentionally stepping all over my feet, throwing me off balance. In an earlier time I would have turned my back and stalked away in anger; but I was finally beginning to realize that perhaps these lessons are given to us for our personal growth.

Joe and I wanted Chris back in school, but we seemed to be fighting a losing battle. He wanted to pursue a career that would use his artistic ability. Specifically, he wanted to be a tattoo artist. This dream seemed be his only goal and finally, in desperation, I phoned a friend—an established tattoo artist who knew many in the industry.

Apprenticeships in that field are almost impossible to get, especially for a young, brash kid who felt he already knew everything. Nevertheless, she was able to convince a friend of hers to take him on as an apprentice, and we were able to come up with the apprenticeship fee.

We were all pleased at how well this experience was going for Chris. His mentor/teacher said Chris seemed to have been born with a tattoo machine in hand, and he progressed rapidly. He soon began to work on customers for pay and was able to purchase a motorcycle. It didn't take long, however, before he had an accident that totaled the motorcycle and injured his leg so he was no longer able to work.

Thus began a spiral in our lives from which we couldn't seem to free ourselves. We plunged repeatedly between hope and trust to doubt and despair as Chris went from being successful as an artist to disaster, from seeming to want to conquer his addiction to diving deeper and deeper into drugs. He succeeded, at our insistence, in getting his GED and then found work in a tattoo shop in California where he seemed to be very successful, only to fritter away those opportunities and lose his job. He moved back to Oregon and asked us to help him with moving costs and to allow him to live with us.

Again he found work easily enough in Oregon and was able to eventually buy the shop, but again his addictions took control and things eventually fell apart. He started a tumultuous relationship with a woman whom we later learned had a drinking problem. They lived together but their constant fighting caused them to be evicted from the apartment they were living in. We allowed them to live with us, until we could no longer stand their fighting and the chaos. She and her daughter moved out, then became homeless and moved back in with us. It was a three-ring-circus, and the lion of addiction was roaring and hungry, waiting to destroy all of us.

Chris' girlfriend Judy finally told us that our son was a heroin addict. For me this was the ultimate horror—the incurable "thing" that caused people to waste their lives away. I could not believe it. I had seen movies, like *The Man with the Golden Arm,* that terrified me, and I knew this was a nightmare that would not go away just by waking up.

We confronted Chris the next day; he admitted the problem and promised to quit but it soon became clear that quitting was not on his agenda. I felt as though God had completely abandoned me once again despite all my prayers and all of my spiritual practice. Even though I had stopped attending Mass years before, I had never stopped praying for Chris, and for what? Things were worse now than ever before.

Judy's daughter Maria kept asking me to take her to church. I was so angry with God I wasn't ready to return to church, so at first I sent her to church with others. I finally relented, found a Catholic Church in my neighborhood and took her to Mass on Palm Sunday. The rituals, the procession with palms, the reading of the Passion all felt so familiar and right. During the Mass I began to cry; it was like coming home.

I started taking Maria every week and finally attended a reconciliation service. I was terrified because I'd been away from the Church for so long. The priest just smiled, patted me on the shoulders and said "welcome back." It was all the encouragement I needed to once again accept the embrace of a Partner who wanted to hold me and guide my steps more closely again.

Maria wanted to join the Church and, after a preparation period, she was baptized the following Easter at the Easter Vigil. Judy was pregnant with our granddaughter and things seemed to be hopeful once again.

Suspecting that Chris was still using drugs, we arranged for an intervention. The intervention brought all of us together: Chris' parents, sister, and grandmothers. We knew Chris would be very embarrassed. He agreed to enter treatment but after a week said he was "fine" and ready to come home.

Hoping he really was well again, we helped Chris, Judy and Maria get into a rental house, and for a while things were okay. When our granddaughter Laura was born, we were thrilled and thought the drug problem was behind us. They brought the new baby home, but soon everything fell apart again and only got worse.

I continued to pray feverishly for him to get into treatment and actually get off the drugs for good. But it felt like God did not care, was not listening.

By then the children were living with us most of the time as Chris and Judy's lives continued to spiral down. I was angry with Chris, and Joe and I argued continually. All this stress led me to a complete nervous breakdown. My doctor put me on medical leave, prescribing medication to help me cope and suggested more counseling.

I was unable to work or do anything except drag myself to the counseling sessions and to my yoga classes. I attended Mass but nothing seemed to have meaning. I almost hated my own son. Forgive him? How? He had stolen money from us and wreaked havoc on our lives for so many years; how could I forgive him?

The counseling helped me understand that chemical dependency—drug addiction and alcoholism—is a disease that needs to be treated. I saw for the first time, through films and conversations with other mothers in my situation, how co-dependent I was and how that might be contributing to the problem.

During this very difficult time, I had a very helpful meditation teacher. He has since passed away, but he was the kindest, most gentle man I had ever met; in fact, I would call him Christ-like. He was a paraplegic so I learned a lot from him about having problems that might seem insurmountable. He reminded me that Christ, Buddha, Mother Teresa—all the people I so admired—taught that we must love and forgive. He also taught me about unconditional love.

I learned to admit and accept that while I really did love Chris, that did not mean I had to approve or disapprove of his actions. His choices were between him and God, and all I could do was continue to love him and pray for him. My teacher taught me that there is a plan for every life and, for whatever reason, this was how Chris would learn the lessons he needed to learn. Okay, I thought, I could love him, but I didn't believe I could ever forgive; he had hurt his family too deeply.

One day, as I was whining about my situation to a good friend, she suggested a book by Jesuit Father

180

Gary Smith, called *Radical Compassion: Finding Christ in the Heart of the Poor*. She thought it would help me put things in a different perspective. After our conversation I forgot all about the book, but next time I saw her she gave me her copy.

Reading *Radical Compassion* opened my eyes about forgiveness and compassion. Father Smith was the pastor at the Downtown Chapel in Portland, where he worked with the drug addicts, alcoholics and mentally ill who live in the Single Room Occupancies—SROs—in downtown Portland. He never judged the people he ministered to. He did not try to fix them or lecture to them or do anything except listen with compassion and be a friend, no matter how much alcohol or drugs they had consumed. It didn't matter if they treated him badly, just like Jesus he continued to visit them in their small rooms in downtown Portland and show them love and care.

Radical Compassion helped me realize and accept that addicts are not in control of their lives—the drugs and alcohol are in control. Father Smith wrote that it is important for family and friends not to hate them but instead to love them, refrain from judging them, and, above all, forgive them. In the words of Christ on the cross: "Father forgive them for they know not what they do." I realized that these words of Christ are especially relevant to addicts; it was a real epiphany for me.

Although it still seemed to me that God had not listened to my prayers and had not been there for me, I kept going back to the *Radical Compassion* book. This was the beginning of my understanding that God ALWAYS answers our prayers—just not in the way we think God should or in the time frame we have set. Above all, I knew in my heart I had to forgive Chris.

Jesus asks—demands actually—that all of us

embrace those whom society, the world, rejects. We are called to love them and treat them with respect as children of God. Jesus' words from the cross "Father, forgive them" mean literally forgive everyone, including ourselves. I learned that I not only had to forgive my son, but I had to forgive myself.

I was working on forgiving Chris when he walked completely out of my life one day. It wasn't unusual for us not to see him for several days but when Judy told me she had not seen him for a week or more, it was very unusual. In spite of his problems, he was good about staying in contact with her and especially with his child, Laura. I became very worried and as the weeks went by without any contact from him, I gave him up and accepted that he was probably dead. I contacted the coroner's office but was assured that he was not there. I prayed that God would take care of him and forgive him. It was all I could do for my son. I had to "let go and let God."

He was gone for about six months, and to this day I have no idea where he was.

When I had all but given up hope of ever seeing or hearing from Chris again, out of the blue one day he called. I asked about the addiction, only to be disappointed with his answer. But remembering what I had learned from *Radical Compassion*, I looked into my heart and forgave him again. One week later, Chris entered a treatment facility and the happy answer to all my prayers finally came.

In September of 2010, we were able to celebrate the fact that he had been clean and sober for six years and is still clean and sober today. He is engaged to a lovely young woman, has full custody of his daughter, Laura, has returned to his profession and is working again. For me it was that long-awaited miracle and only God can work miracles.

Chris had tried the treatment route so many

times but had never stayed; he always came out too soon and returned to his old lifestyle. Chris has shared with me he does not know why he stayed and "made it" this time, but I know. God and his Blessed Mother and St. Jude answered my prayers, the prayers of a heartbroken mother.

Christ forgave all of us. Mary did the same, even able to forgive the people who killed her son. Can we do less? On my faith journey, I have been in and out of the Church and of spiritual practice countless times, but God had not ever really let me go, even when I tried to dance far away. When Chris actually went into treatment, stayed there and really got his life back, I realized that God had been with me all along on this difficult journey; God had listened to my pleas and answered them, in God's time and in God's way.

Joe has also remained sober and is a wonderful husband. We now have a beautiful marriage. Joe has finally found it in his heart to forgive Chris, another miracle! Chris and his fiancé will be married this summer.

My life is a joyful celebration dance after so many years of struggle, and I am filled with gratitude. It is my hope that someday I can help someone else, another mother with a child having problems, and pay back these gifts that have been given to me by a generous, loving, forgiving God.

God Writes Straight
With Crooked Lines

Written Anonymously
by a woman who could be your friend, sister,
aunt, mother or daughter

He was teaching in a synagogue on the Sabbath. And a woman was there who for eighteen years had been crippled by a spirit; she was bent over, completely incapable of standing erect. When Jesus saw her, he called to her and said "Woman, you are set free of your infirmity." He laid his hands on her, and she at once stood up straight and glorified God. – Luke 13: 10-12

ONE OF LIFE'S PARADOXES is that the search for love and acceptance often leads us on dark paths of lies, guilt and self-hatred.

Growing up in the Midwest in a large family, I figured out early on how to get along. I smiled, laid low and cooperated. My mom has told me that I was such a good baby, always a good girl and rarely gave my parents any trouble. I had learned that behaving a certain way gained me the approval I desired, and—as it was for many children of my generation—receiving approval from my parents and others was a way of measuring my worth.

My father had a very strong personality and enjoyed being the center of attention. My father, a convert to Catholicism, followed all the rules and guidelines for being a "good Catholic" and taught us to value them, as well. He was very protective of us all, including my mother, a quiet and sensitive person who allowed few people to be close to her.

My parents were affectionate with each other, but not so much with their children, which was probably standard for the time period. I was 35 the first time I remember hearing the words "I love you" from my parents. I now realize that that was how they were raised. But growing up, I believed love had to be earned.

My siblings and I all attended Catholic grade and high school. In grade school, I honed my skills of earning approval and love and became known as an "apple polisher." I volunteered to help the nuns by cleaning blackboards or carrying their big leather satchels full of papers and books back to the convent each day after school. This brought me the affirmation I craved and helped bolster my fragile sense of self-worth.

At the all-girls' high school I attended, I soon learned that simply cooperating and getting along with people wasn't rewarded as I had come to expect; being good didn't seem to matter as much as I'd believed. I discovered that girls just as smart as or smarter than me were able to succeed without being nice.

High school was a confusing time. My mom discouraged me from being too close to my friends, telling me that one could only trust the family. But I didn't feel very close to my family. In many ways I was a typical teenager, experiencing all the regular teenage joys and sorrows. It seemed that all my friends had boyfriends, and having a boyfriend myself became a major focus in my life. I measured my self-worth by how many dates I had and bargained with God for popularity, promising to go to Mass every day if certain boys would like me.

When I was a senior in high school, one of my sisters became pregnant. My parents were mortified. I remember my own humiliation and shame of trying to cover it up and to explain why my sister had gotten married so quickly. A few years earlier, another sister had also gotten pregnant, and my parents' concern to both pregnancies seemed to be what other people would think about them, how they might be judged as inadequate parents.

In spite of my mother's advice, I became an accomplished follower, staying in the background and going along with no questions asked, often feeling as though I was fading into the woodwork. My self-worth was so dependent on being accepted by my friends that I was unable to say no. I joined my friends in drinking alcohol before football games, and at parties we chain-smoked cigarettes, feeling it made us look cool. Somehow I never got caught in these antics, but participating in behaviors I knew my parents would not approve of made it more challenging to continue my charade of the dutiful daughter.

I enrolled in the local junior college, continuing to live at home and working part-time to pay my tuition. It seemed like the sensible, responsible way to move forward with my life; but I continued to follow my friends in risky behavior to fit in. It was during my college years that I experienced an episode that would shape and color my self-image and self-worth for many years to come.

It seemed to me I was the only person in the world who wasn't in love. All my friends were either married or seriously dating, and my heart had been broken a few times. I felt inadequate and unloved and stifled. I was 22 and desperate to find someone to appreciate me.

Then it happened: I began dating man I was working with. I fell in love and desperately wanted to believe that he was the right man for me; I was willing to do whatever he asked to win his love. I learned too late that he was not good for me and when the relationship ended, I felt totally worthless. But by then I was pregnant. Remembering the experiences of my two sisters, I didn't trust that my parents would continue to love me if I, too, were pregnant. I couldn't risk their rejection. I decided the best solution to my situation was to get an abortion.

My whole life had been based on pleasing people and being good. I didn't know how to deal with the truth that I had not only let down my parents, but myself.

Soon after the abortion I sought counseling and was able to mend on the surface. I moved into my own apartment over the protests of my dad, who tried to insist I stay at home until I was safely married. After leaving home, I stopped going to church, which only added to my guilt. I switched jobs, made new friends, and began to recover. My self-esteem began to blossom.

When I met the man who was to become my husband and it appeared that my future was secured, my family and friends breathed a sigh of relief (and I suppose that I did as well!). We married and began our family. Those years of babies and diapers kept me in a state of constant busy-ness and allowed me to block out my college experience as an unfortunate incident. I had gone to confession before our wedding not only because I regretted my abortion, but also because I believed confession would square things with the Church and God.

Religion returned to my life. My husband and I attended church regularly, and I experienced my spiritual life in a new way. We prayed together, my husband taking the lead; his thoughts and prayers seemed so much more inspired than mine. I was impressed with his responsibility to our family and the Church. Once again I was living the image of the "good girl," the dutiful daughter, loving wife and responsible, good mother. We had become the image of a good, Catholic family; we were active in the parish and all seemed well again.

In June 1990 my sister was diagnosed with cancer, living only a few months after the diagnosis. She left three children from two marriages. In spite of the chaos of her life, my sister had a terrific sense of humor and extraordinary courage. It didn't seem fair to me that my sister, who had endured two abusive husbands, should have to suffer and die as she did. Her death triggered a spiral of guilt and grief in my heart and soul.

My sister had made several bad choices in her life and had paid dearly for them. I had come through my own mistakes seemingly unscathed and undetected by family and the world. I began to question God and my own self-worth. I developed psychosomatic illnesses— chest pains, headaches, panic attacks—you name it. Through counseling I again tried to get my act together. I tried medication, meditation, and read every self-help book I could get my hands on. My search was ongoing. My friends were endlessly sympathetic and kind, even though they did not know the true source of my unhappiness and grief.

Several years later my husband and I were asked to help coordinate a renewal week. Accepting this invitation, we met a priest and sister from a nearby retreat center. They inspired me and I admired their peace-filled presence. I was intrigued to learn that they offered a retreat program for individuals—called a spiritual growth community—that met several times each year for a three-year journey into the soul.

After a year of excuses and continued anxiety, I finally joined the process. At the end of each weekend away I returned to my life full of enthusiasm and courage. Usually by noon the next day with the kids fighting and laundry piled sky high, I was back to my own reality. I was still trying to hold it all together on my own, with God's help in emergencies. It was so difficult for me to trust, to believe in God's unconditional love for me.

Praying alone was not central to my life at this time, and praying with my husband didn't hold the same magic as before. The very strength and faith that had attracted me to him before now distanced me from him. I resented him and what I perceived as his control over me.

At the time, some friends were in the process of adopting a little girl from a single young woman. I knew how thrilled they were, and I was racked with guilt and remorse for not displaying that courage in my own life. At Easter that year I even confessed my abortion again.

Reconciliation left me exhausted from crying but peaceful. My ongoing spiritual work did not result in any grand revelations or visions that would instantly change my life. Rather, little by little, in my own mixed up way I was becoming aware of the gift of healing grace in my life. At one of my weekend retreats, one of the speakers quoted from Psalm 95. The words seemed to cut through my all thoughts and I clung to them as one would a life preserver: "If today you hear God's voice, harden not your heart." I believed God was speaking words of consolation and love to me, if only I could be open to them.

I had been clinging to the safety of my old life, despite the pain it caused me, simply because change seemed even more painful. The very idea of telling others about my past filled me with fear of rejection, but finally I realized opening my heart meant letting others in and that would be a way of letting God in. I decided to take the risk and confided in two friends. I had known one for years but the other I'd only known for a few months. I recognized God's presence in their lives, and they listened with open hearts. I could see God's love and compassion in their eyes and felt the weight of the fear that had kept me prisoner for so many years falling off my shoulders. God was not giving up on me.

The next stage of my journey of healing came when our parish pastoral minister asked me to work for her while she recovered from surgery. My duties included taking Communion to the homebound and visiting hospitalized parishioners. The work was very humbling, and when it ended I found myself continuing to look to the daily readings for inspiration. Thus began my habit of sitting quietly each morning, and reflecting on the Word, knowing that God is with us every step of the way, guiding us through the forks in the road, calming our fears, forgiving our sins, loving us unconditionally.

Over the ensuing 15 years, I've continued to learn from this experience. Following are a few of the lessons that have been given to me, and I hope they can help others in making peace with and letting go of past mistakes.

I have learned that the journey to healing is very long, and guilt is a roadblock that prevents your arrival.

Years ago I presented my story for the first time at a women's retreat. At the completion of my talk one of the participants confided that she had been carrying around a similar "bag of garbage" for almost 30 years. I felt shocked and sad for her, unwilling to comprehend that she had been unable to find peace in all that time. I wondered what else could be said or done to accomplish the task of healing from deep hurts, including those things we have done to harm ourselves. And why would there be any further need, after 25 or 30 years? Giving a presentation to a small group of women a thousand miles from my home seemed like a safe start for me. I wondered what this woman needed to do? I hoped that her journey of healing would begin soon.

As I soon realized, I was just beginning my own work. In spite of all my efforts, each year around the anniversary of my abortion I still experienced a great sadness that only subsided after conversations with my spiritual director. She listened and prayed with me, assured me of God's love, and encouraged me to consider the diocesan program for post-abortion trauma.

Right on cue, last year in early spring I began to feel such deep sadness that I sought out professional counseling for what I thought must be depression. Working on many levels of my anxiety, my counselor and I explored my grief and recalled the abortion event and what I remembered from that painful day.

Coincidentally, during that time I attended a production of *Les Miserables*, based on Victor Hugo's novel, a beautiful story of redemption, love and forgiveness. After a life of running and hiding from his past, Jean Valjean lies dying, and Fantine sings to him "lay down your burden" and "come with me, where chains will never bind you, your grief will be behind you." Tears streamed down my face as I found myself immersed in the moment and witnessing the cleansing effects of peace in the soul. As Victor Hugo wrote, "To love another is to see the face of God."

A few days later I experienced an incredibly healing dream. In it I saw a little girl with a blond curl on the top of her head, a head that was quite large and strangely shaped. She was very odd looking. I could sense a presence next to me and the little girl. I wasn't sure where we were, but the presence was feminine. The little girl was smiling at me, a loving and accepting smile; and it seemed to me there was also forgiveness in her smile. The presence kept saying in a soft voice: "Isn't she a beautiful little girl?"

When I awoke from the dream I wondered if that presence might have been God Herself and if this child was my own little girl who was bringing me a message of love and forgiveness. I felt comforted that she was not annihilated; she was at peace with God who loved her very much. Her little spirit could not be destroyed. I felt peace knowing my child is happy and loved.

This dream has made all the difference in guiding me toward healing and peace.

I realize that my image of God and my faith are continuing to evolve.

My willingness to accept forgiveness has helped me to see myself as a person of value and worth. In turn, grace enables me to trust in and envision a loving God. The experience of God as feminine in my dream symbolizes my desire to know God more fully, to go beyond my child-like idea of God as judge in the clouds.

Several years ago, in reading author Sue Monk Kidd's *The Dance of the Dissident Daughter,* I was surprised at and curious about the challenge toward a new level of feminine spiritual consciousness. Her earlier book, *When the Heart Waits* concerns the slow, patient walk of spiritual growth, and I found it to be a comforting message. Now I am challenged to think about God in a new way, to think of myself as made in the image of God; and as a woman, that means a feminine perspective of a comforting God.

While the message of my upbringing was to lay low and not ask questions, I now feel compelled to reconsider the patriarchal faith tradition of our Church, the injustice that prevents women from ordination, and the hierarchy that refuses to guide the Church toward a transformation which will acknowledge and honor the spiritual gifts of women.

My search has been cyclical; often I'm unsure where I'm headed. But as with the beauty of the changing seasons, I am assured of my Creator's presence and promise. God wants me to open my heart, soul and being to grow, think, pray, love and stretch myself each day of my life.

The following poem by Kaylin Haught, used with permission, sums up my new understanding of God:

God Says Yes to me
I asked God if it was okay to be melodramatic
And she said yes
I asked her if it was okay to be short
And she said it sure is
I asked her if I could wear nail polish
Or not wear nail polish
And she said honey
She calls me that sometimes
She said you can do exactly
What you want to do
Thanks God I said
And is it even okay if I don't paragraph

My letters
Sweetcakes God said
Who knows where she picked that up
What I'm telling you is
Yes Yes Yes

© Kaylin Haught

I realize I am not in this alone.

I see my life as an example of the Spanish proverb: "God writes straight with crooked lines." With deep regret and repentance, I acknowledge my many mistakes along the way. Yet my choices, so often the source of great pain and sorrow, have molded me into who I am today. I can't escape my past problems or my own brokenness, and sometimes it seems so easy to slip back into the old ways of self-defeating thoughts and behavior. But God has remained with me through my offenses and mistakes, both large and small, by being faithful and offering the grace of insight and healing. Many times this grace arrives through something I read or an image of peacefulness and beauty in nature. But most often I find God's presence through the kindness, loyalty and friendship of others. I can know God's love because we humans share a tiny fragment of that goodness with each other. And I am blessed and truly grateful.

Finding the Grace in Loneliness

by Maureen Hovenkotter

*Perhaps the painful awareness of loneliness
. . . is a gift we must protect and guard,
because our loneliness reveals to us an inner
emptiness that can be . . . filled with promise
for those who can tolerate its sweet pain.
-- Henri J. M. Nouwen*

WHEN I was a young girl attending Catholic grade school, our class was sometimes asked to sing at funerals. I still remember some of the solemn Latin chants we sang: "Dies iræ! dies illa, solvet sæclum in favilla . . ." We sang at one particularly poignant requiem mass for an elderly woman: our class and the celebrant were the only ones present. This seemed to me to be one of the most painful experiences: to have no one who loved or cared about you enough to mourn your passing, to have your life count for so little that no one came to say goodbye.

What did she do to become so alone? I wondered as a girl. *She must have been unpleasant, selfish or done hurtful things. Why else would no one love her? Didn't she have family who cared about her?* It's so easy to judge others without knowing their stories. At that tender age, surrounded by people at school and home every waking minute, and sharing a bedroom with my sister every night (not always amicably), I couldn't imagine being alone for any length of time. The possibility that I might be counted among those lonely people one day never occurred to me; or perhaps it registered but I buried that fear somewhere deep inside.

Over the many years since that lonely funeral I attended as a girl, the fear of dying alone and unloved lay dormant, but occasionally it bubbled up into my conscious thought. I recall conversations—half in jest full in earnest—with friends regarding who would have the most (or the fewest) people at our funerals. This gallows humor was possibly a type of bravado, laughing in the face of a death we assumed was still off in some distant future. But it was also a way of sharing our vulnerability, our hopes that we would never die unloved, unmourned and unremembered.

The truth is our culture often measures how beloved or valued someone was by the number of people who attend his or her funeral. Even after death, life is still apparently something of a popularity contest. I doubt the dead really care how many attend their funerals and probably aren't worrying about who loves them. When we die I expect we all will know how very much we are loved and that it has never been a contest. Perhaps we will finally realize we're all winners. I understand now that funerals are primarily to comfort the survivors: rituals to say goodbye and reassure those who are left that their loved one was also loved by others, that his or her life had meaning and value.

A couple years after high school I married, going from my family of birth to my family of choice. I assumed marriage would assure me of companionship. John and I both came from large families; even before our two children were born, I was sure we would always have family around. We had careers, we had friends, we had our faith community and life felt safe and companionable. It wasn't perfect because no life is perfect; but it was good and it was meaningful. I loved my husband, I loved my children, and I knew that they loved, appreciated and needed me.

Life was often too busy and stressful, juggling the demands of a career and the needs of a husband and children. Sometimes it felt like there was never time for me, and the idea of being a hermit, living alone on a mountain somewhere—at least for a month or two—looked like an attractive alternative to my crazy life. I looked forward to the future when John and I could watch our son and daughter build their own lives and families and have time to pursue our own dreams. In retrospect, I now realize I didn't yet understand the value of living in and appreciating the present moment.

One of the hard lessons I have learned is that my assumptions about how life will unfold have little to do with reality. Having expectations, believing in certain specific outcomes, is the quickest way for me to be disappointed, frustrated, sad or angry. According to my plan, John and I should be happily retired as some of our friends are, enjoying the fruits of our labors together, playing with grandchildren, traveling, exploring things we'd always wanted to do but never had the time or money to before.

All those expectations for the future were shattered, along with so much in my life, when John was killed suddenly in an accident nearly eight years ago. I had never imagined John would die before me. I wasn't prepared to be alone; after 33 years of marriage, I had no training and no frame of reference for it. Loneliness became an ongoing presence in my life, a companion I was never comfortable with.

For the first three-and-a-half years after John's death, I continued to work at my job as an aide to a U.S. Senator. This provided me the companionship of great co-workers and a sense of purpose. I had a reason to get up every morning. I felt important and valued. I had meaningful work that often made a real difference in people's lives. Although it seemed like the right decision at the time, and I'm still not convinced it was wrong, in 2007 I made a well-considered choice to leave that job and take early retirement to pursue other interests. I believed I needed time to read, write, paint, travel, and solitude to pray and figure out my life. It was again that pull to do something for me, to follow a deeper yearning, only this time nothing was holding me back.

After a few months, it became clear that the absence of daily contact with friends at work, added to the loss of a sense of purpose, made the hole in my life left by John's death even larger and more difficult to ignore. I discovered that, at least in my case, Loneliness has a twin sister: Irrelevance. She shows up in my fear that I don't matter, that I am insignificant, have nothing to contribute and little to show for my time on earth. In my darkest hours she whispers devastating, self-pitying questions: if I were to cease to exist tomorrow, would anyone notice, or care? Would anyone be there to mourn my passing or remember me? Would anyone miss me?

Our culture's emphasis on pragmatism and production leads us to believe that our value in the world is measured by what we do. We feel compelled to continually do more, do better. Outside of our accomplishments, we seem to believe we have little worth. If we can't show others our trophies or degrees or certificates of recognition, if we don't have impressive accomplishments or titles to share, how will anyone know our value? How will we believe it ourselves? Since I retired I have few measurable outcomes to prove to myself and the world that I am using my gifts to help others or make a difference.

The two roles that had most completely defined my adult life—wife and mother—no longer apply at all or are significantly diminished. My two adult children, now married, live their own busy lives, one in another state and the other several hours away. Of course they would miss me if I were no longer in their lives, just as deeply as they miss their father. I know my passing would be very painful to them. But on a day-to-day basis, they no longer need me much.

Perhaps the missing ingredient in my life that I often find most distressing is the recognition that I'm no longer special to anyone, that I'm no one's "only one." In addition to missing the romance and physical connection—touch and passion—the loss of the deep companionship and intimate understanding that a long-term love relationship brings can be very painful. The longing I feel when I see other couples my age together, obviously enjoying each other's company, is as sharp as the hunger pangs I sometimes felt growing up in a large family with a small income. It is both physical and emotional pain.

A television ad currently running features older people sharing their dreams about retirement, things they still want to do. One woman confides she wants to fall in love again. *Wouldn't that be nice*, I tell myself as I watch the ad, *especially if it was a mutual falling-in-love*. I know this is not impossible, because anything is possible with God, but I am coming to accept that my journey may lie in another direction. At least for now.

In *The Holy Longing: The Search for a Christian Spirituality,* Ronald Rolheiser, a Catholic priest and well-known spiritual writer, refers to "celibacy by conscription." He writes there is "a real poverty, a painful searing one" for those who are forced by circumstance rather than choice to "sleep alone."

It certainly has not escaped my attention that, as Rolheiser writes, "the universe works in pairs." It sometimes feels that if you are not part of a couple, you are indeed living outside "the norm for human intimacy," and it can be a very painful experience. In the creation story related in Genesis (2:18), "the Lord God said: It is not good for the man to live alone." Later, God instructed Noah to bring the animals onto the ark in pairs. So what is God thinking, I wonder, that I—and so many others—are alone. It's no wonder I sometimes feel a bit like an outsider, excluded.

When Loneliness and Irrelevance start to gang up on me, one way to silence them is by refocusing and reframing, changing my perspective, finding meaning in my life as it is now. So much of my personal pain is a result of how I view challenges, how I think about my circumstances. If I think of my loneliness as punishment, I will rebel against the pain. If I base my value on what I accomplish and measure my worth on the positive recognition and admiration of others, I will always fall short of satisfaction. No one can make me feel worthwhile if I cannot see myself as inherently valuable. Remembering how greatly beloved I am by the One who created me is really the only true way to measure my worth.

The more I focus on the hard places in my life, the more pain they bring. Instead of listening to the false stories my ego tells me, I can choose to dissect those lies and find the truth. Sometimes it's as simple as finding the beauty, the gift in everything. I think if we look hard enough for the good, we will find it. Focusing my eyes on the abundance of my life helps me feel blessed and grateful.

When I reflect on the positives, I realize that though it's true I spend more hours and days alone than I would prefer, I also have strong social connections. I don't see my daughter as often as I'd like, but I speak to her on the phone at least once a week. My son, who lives a little closer, comes to visit more often, usually bringing my darling grandson along. Sometimes they help me with little projects, sometimes we just share time being together. It feels helpful having loved ones present and part of my life, which reminds me that my presence in their lives makes a difference to them.

I am incredibly blessed with a number of close friends and confidants with whom I can share many of my struggles, questions, fears, hopes and dreams, not to mention plenty of laughter. I have frequent phone conversations with my two sisters, though both live too far away to spend "face time" with regularly. I do spend time nearly every week with a brother who lives in Portland. We often walk my golden retriever Charlie, sometimes enjoy cooking together, and he helps with challenges like setting rat traps or disposing of "mostly dead" possums I find in my yard—the joys of living in the suburbs.

Many of my friends are dealing with elderly parents who need time, care and attention. I listen as they share these challenges, the stress and pain in their voices unmistakable. The relief that I feel in being spared some of the decisions they face is a two-edged sword. I have already walked that path with my parents. My mother died of breast cancer 15 years ago, and my father passed away the year after John. Their deaths left additional holes in my life, but the fact that I still miss them years later reminds me that even though I no longer have an active role in helping my children, they would indeed miss me.

My most constant companion is Charlie, who loves me without ever judging me and needs me, giving me purpose. He is delighted to be the recipient of my need for touch and will sit for hours as I pet him, rub his ears, scratch his belly, as long as I have the strength and patience to continue. He is never reticent about asking for attention and affection, a lesson to me of the value of being vulnerable and asking for emotional support when I need it. He gets me out into the world for regular walks, which often lead to at least brief exchanges with others, usually about what a beautiful dog Charlie is. He's easy to plan meals for, never complains, and doesn't expect to have any say in what music we listen to or what we watch on television. On the other hand, he snores and steals covers, shoes and anything else he can carry away, so he is rarely allowed in my bedroom.

When I feel sad about my lack of a partner, I can admit the truth: I could have remarried, but it was neither the right time nor the right partner. I know too many people who, despite being married or in a relationship, are still incredibly lonely. I have friends who are unhappy but unable to make the difficult decision of ending a relationship that is not life giving. It seems easier to hold onto the security of a hell they already know. Perhaps having someone to fight with seems less intimidating than being alone. I am willing to remain single rather than marry the wrong person for the wrong reason, and the longer I am alone, the more comfortable I am with that path.

My strong belief in a Creator who loves me without reservations and with whom I communicate often, along with active participation in a supportive faith community, have been incredibly helpful to me, especially after losing John. Franciscan priest and modern mystic Richard Rohr writes in *Everything*

Belongs: The Gift of Contemplative Prayer, "God is a lover. Prayer is being loved at a deep, sweet level."

At times when the sadness of lying alone in bed seems unbearable, I have imagined God wrapping arms around me in a loving embrace, whispering how beloved I am. Trusting that God's love and presence is enough is hard, but I have come to accept it is the only way I will ever truly fulfill the deep need and longing for connection that is beyond the ability of any human to meet. On the plus side, in my experience God, unlike Charlie, does not snore or steal the covers.

These blessings in my life are all deterrents to chronic loneliness, and I am very thankful for them. Even recalling all these gifts, I still find it challenging to let go of my ego needs for positive recognition and approval from others. And I still struggle with finding a sense of purpose.

This past year I served on a committee to develop a new volunteer opportunity for older adults. The program, affiliated with Jesuit Volunteer Corps Northwest, is known as Jesuit Volunteer EnCorps (or JVE). This fall it will begin to provide opportunities for volunteers aged 50 and older to use the skills and experience they've developed to continue to contribute in various ways. A key component to this program is ongoing spiritual support throughout the year-long commitment. This has led me to explore and discern volunteer opportunities that are meaningful to me and respond to a deep desire to make a difference rather than a frantic need to fill empty hours or feel important.

When I reflect on my role with this committee, it was primarily one of instigator, of listening to the needs of other recently retired people and then encouraging the sponsoring agency's executive director to begin and convene this exploratory committee. Since then, it was primarily one of accompaniment on the committee's journey, contributing my presence, support and occasional thoughts or reflections as a recently retired person. At times I found my inadequate organizational and management skills frustrating and believed I wasn't contributing much to move the idea forward to fruition. But friends on the committee assured me that offering my life perspective and my spiritual insights did indeed make a difference: just being there to listen and provide feedback helped, they said.

My spiritual director often reminds me that accompaniment—being present and supportive to others in their journey—is a skill that not everyone is willing or able to develop. He encourages me to accept that skill as a gift to myself and others. Being present to people, being a supportive, listening friend on their journey is not an impressive skill or one our culture values very highly. But it is a way of mirroring God's love and presence in our lives, of modeling God for others. Many people believe in a God who pulls strings, manipulates reality, answers our prayers like a magic genii. This is not the God I have come to know on my spiritual journey.

All my life I have felt pulled into deeper union with a loving God who is present with us, comforting us, whispering how deeply loved we are, as we face our human challenges. God is more than a cheerleader; God understands the challenges because God became human in the person of Jesus, and experienced all the light and dark, the joy and suffering, and life and death we all must face at some point. Through Jesus, God experienced being outcast, misjudged, unappreciated, lonely. Through Jesus, God journeyed with the outsiders, those who didn't fit in, weren't acceptable company, were excluded from bragging rights and impressive accomplishments.

God is in solidarity with my struggles and difficulties because God has experienced that pain through Jesus. Facing my own suffering and trying to mirror my response to the suffering modeled by God-made-man helps me find the grace in it. This "new attitude" and "new self created to be like God" (Ephesians 4:23-24) allows me to be more compassionate, more present to others in their suffering. Spiritual writers call this redemptive suffering or "compassio," and it has powerful potential to be life giving.

My new self is still under construction. Learning to make peace with my role of widow, to live in the tension of loneliness and find ways to give my life meaning and purpose again has taken years. Despite times in the past when I longed for this gift of solitude, I now sometimes find it painful. There are times my journey feels incredibly dark and empty. And thankless. Perhaps it will always feel incomplete. But that, too, is a lesson: learning to accept that we may never know whom we have touched and what our lives mean to others.

One of the blessings of true maturity is acknowledging that we no longer have to prove anything to anyone; that we cannot control most of what happens in our lives but only how we respond to life. We can stop worrying about how we look to others and start actually looking through loving eyes at all around us. We learn to let go of things, not take them so seriously, to stop judging and comparing. We learn to be thankful for the many gifts we have received and put aside our wish-lists and our expectations for more. We become less driven and more willing to be. Those are gifts of beauty that can come to humans in the autumn of their lives. But getting there requires change, and the ego hates change, especially when it means the ego must go on a diet and lose part of itself. It is a painful refining process.

The faith journey I have chosen to follow the last few years has been inspired by the mystics, those who have come to know God through experience of prayer and listening, detachment from the world. It is not an easy path to follow, one filled with dryness, sacrifice, suffering.

Starting with the Desert Fathers and Mothers of the Third Century, mystics have often chosen a life of solitude, living separately in hermitages, working and praying alone much of the time. Often they saw this as a type of martyrdom, death of the need for comfort, gratification, and selfish, narcissistic pursuits.

The Spanish mystic John of the Cross wrote of the Dark Night of the Senses and Spirit, a process of stripping our lives of the curtains that keep us from seeing with the eyes of Christ and finding union with God. This transformation requires letting go of ego gratification needs, abandoning old pieces of ourselves that are no longer needed. It requires reconciling with shadow parts that have been long buried because they are threats to the ego. It's a way of lightening the load for the further journey.

A new Christ-inspired attitude can help me appreciate the sometimes-challenging gift of solitude. Walking the lonesome valley I find myself in can help me lose my sense of who I am based on "purpose," contribution, my value as I think others view it. This Dark Night of the Soul experience helps me begin the process of losing myself to find God. Finding a balance between solitude and meaningful connections, between being and doing, is a difficult challenge. I recognize that the compulsion to surround myself with activity and noise is a distraction that keeps me from closer union with God, an impediment to contemplation, the deep prayer of silent listening. By learning to appreciate my time alone, I can find fulfillment and joy in the hours I am able to spend lost in my thoughts and prayers.

Why would anyone choose to follow a path filled with suffering, loss and sacrifice? For the same reason one might be willing to make sacrifices for someone they love, someone who loves them. I feel called on this journey, drawn by love, almost like it wasn't me who chose this path, rather that I was invited. I'm finally learning that each failure, disappointment, unfulfilled expectation and painful loss is another step toward the surrender of self necessary to move forward on my journey. Maybe some day I will even be able to welcome them as blessings.

I am convinced that life is a mystery, and we have no idea what might be just around the corner. I am also convinced that God loves us and will give us what we need. It takes living in tension, accepting we are not in control, and living out of trust in that love that will bring us all we need. As the medieval mystic Julian of Norwich wrote: "Let nothing disturb you. Let nothing frighten you. Everything passes away except God."

Contributors

Barbara Underwood Scharff co-authored with her mother the book *Hostage To Heaven* (Crown/Potter, NY, 1979), an account of Barbara's four years in the Moonie cult and the rescue by her family through a celebrated court trial and deprogramming. She has written for *BabyTalk; The Oakland Tribune* and *The California Journal*. A graduate of the University of California, Berkeley, she worked as producer of a drive-time talk show, celebrity show and public affairs shows at NBC radio in San Francisco in the 1980's. She was a founding board member of *Friends of Trees* and helped organize several field campaigns for parks, schools and candidates in Portland, Oregon. She currently serves as an officer on the board of the *Jesuit Volunteer Corps Northwest* and is a government affairs assistant to Jim Francesconi. She is married to attorney Gary Scharff and has three adult children, Elana, Jesse and Thomas.

Karen Nettler is a native Oregonian and was a manager in social services for the state of Oregon for 30 years. She is a trained inter-denominational spiritual director and is currently in a Spiritual Formation certificate program at George Fox Seminary. She is active in social and economic justice issues in Oregon.

Marie Goretti Abijuru is U.S. citizen from Rwanda. She lives in Portland with her three children and works for the Immigrant and Refugee Community Organization (IRCO). She enjoys working with the conflict resolution team, and helps other refugees and immigrants settle into their new home. She was named Person of the Year for 2009 by the Pacific Northwest Rwandan Association, and accepted the award with sincere appreciation and commitment for the Rwandan Community here in Oregon. She is a member of St. Ignatius parish where she serves on the Pastoral Council and volunteers as a Eucharistic Minister.

Rev. Cheryl Rohret is the minister of Unity Spiritual Life Center in Yakima, WA. She came to Unity in 2005, saying "yes" to serving Unity of Yakima just one week after marking the 25th anniversary of her ordination as a Presbyterian minister. She was ordained in Unity in April of 2010. For her, these changes are simply another fascinating turn on the labyrinth of her life. She loves labyrinths and was trained by the Rev. Dr. Lauren Artress as a labyrinth facilitator. She also loves accompanying people on their spiritual paths and is a certified spiritual director. And she loves encouraging and inspiring others through storytelling and teaching in her spiritual community and beyond. In addition to her ministry, she enjoys reading, traveling, eating out, walking, and spending time with friends doing all of the above.

Katie Hennessy is a Licensed Clinical Social Worker in Portland, Oregon. While employed at Women's Intercommunity AIDS Resource in the 1990's, she joined great and caring others in the co-creation of Camp Starlight, an Epiphanic and sustaining program for children impacted by HIV disease. She holds degrees from Gonzaga University and the Graduate School of Social Work at Portland State University yet feels her greatest teachers are her husband Tim, her three adult children, and her relationships with all of them. She has turned the Crucifix spotlights on most Saturday mornings since 1999 as Presider of Liturgies of the Word with Holy Communion at St. Ignatius Catholic Church, a Jesuit Parish.

Suzanne Dillard Burke grew up in St. Louis but moved to Oregon after graduating from the University of Missouri with a degree in journalism. She earned a master's degree in public administration from the University of Oregon, which led to a career in state government, including time as a manager of energy programs. She has a five-year-old grandson and lives near Portland with her three cats. She enjoys travel and gardening.

Karen Gatens is a mother, creative director/ designer, pranic healer, eclectic Catholic, sometimes-journal-writer and seeker. Living in Portland, Oregon, with two canaries, she struggles to make great coffee. If she had been guided properly, she would have pursued a degree in comparative religions, but instead received a BA in Art. Today she operates a design/ marketing communications firm with emphasis of educational institutions and small business. Favorite quote: "If you always do what you've always done, you'll always get what you've always gotten." She was heard to have muttered, "Is this my process or am I stuck?"

Sherold Barr is a change pioneer and trailblazer for women entrepreneurs and is at the forefront when it comes to teaching women how to re-engineer their lives (www.SheroldBarr.com). Whether you're on this planet to build a meaningful and prosperous life or to create a socially conscious business, Sherold is a master. She's a certified coach with "best-known life coach in America" Martha Beck, a facilitator in The Institute of The Work of Byron Katie, and the founder of WomenHealtheWorld.com.

Lola Scobey is an award-winning writer and a consultant to innovators, entrepreneurs, and non-profits spearheading positive change. In 1985, she co-founded Audio-Therapy Innovations, which pioneered the use of recorded music therapy for children with medical and special needs. Currently, she focuses on the intersection of spirituality and sustainability and is a certified Sustainability Advisor and a certified Spiritual Director.

Marilyn Kirvin has worked as a hospital chaplain, college campus minister, parish pastoral associate, and psychotherapist. She was a co-founder and staff member of the Jesuit Spirituality Center in Portland, working for ten years as a retreat facilitator and spiritual director. She earned a Master of Divinity from Weston Jesuit School of Theology and a Master of Social Work from the University of Wisconsin-Milwaukee. Marilyn is the mother of two wonderful sons, and these days she is spending time writing and appreciating the great gift of living in Oregon.

Gale Cunningham is a network news writer and veteran broadcast journalist whose award-winning reports have aired from radio stations throughout the northwest, to networks including CBS and Westwood One. A lifelong Catholic Christian, Cunningham lives near Portland, Oregon, and is the mother of a grown son.

Marilyn Jaeger Veomett is a life-long learner and educator with advanced degrees in developmental biology and educational psychology. She lives in Portland, Oregon, with her husband, George.

Beth Patterson has a BA in elementary education and an MA in religion from Iliff School of Theology in Denver. Her experience includes more than 20 years in end-of-life care at hospices in Florida and Colorado. She's learned at the feet of two groups of people: those who know that they are dying, and those who don't. She can relate to both groups. Beth has pioneered support and educational programs related to wellness and healing for children and adults; and developed programs specifically for persons living with AIDS, their caregivers and bereaved loved ones. For the past few years, Beth has been an administrator for a child abuse advocacy center and a council on aging. She hosts a multi-blogger website, *The Virtual Teahouse* (virtualteahouse.com) focused on engaging the spirituality of everyday life. She also is a spiritual companion at *Finding Ground* (findingground.com) a service for companioning and developing personal ceremonies for people in life transitions. She lives in Bend, Oregon.

Gayle Yamasaki, a fourth generation Japanese American, was born in Hilo on the Big Island of Hawaii. When she was six, her family moved to Japan, the home of her ancestors. She worked as a counselor in American Samoa, renewing her love of the ocean and beginning a career in higher education that took her on a 33-year journey from counselor/storycatcher to fundraiser/grants writer. Her love of water and the natural world brought her to discover the joys of snorkeling, swimming and kayaking. She is currently working on an oral history project recording the stories of Japanese Americans who were incarcerated at the Tule Lake segregation center during WWII. Her focus has been on the stories of women and those who were considered disloyal. Thus her role as a story catcher continues. She lives in Klamath Falls, Oregon.

Charlotte Bloebaum lives in Portland, where she worked at a large independent bookstore for a number of years. Prior to that, she taught dance and both Hatha & Kundalini yoga for many years, a vocation she hopes to return to one day. She loves Scottish Terriers and cats, and currently has two Scotties now after losing one earlier this year. She has two beautiful grandchildren.

Maureen Hovenkotter has written about faith and spiritual matters for a number of publications, including The Oregonian, The National Catholic Reporter, St. Anthony Messenger and The Catholic Sentinel. In the fall of 2003, her husband of 33 years was killed in an accident. She wrote about that experience and the subsequent pilgrimage journey to discover herself in *42 States of Grace: A Woman's Journey*, (Gray Wings Press, LLC, 2010). She shares her reflections on life and spirituality in her blog, www.travelinwithCharlie.com. The mother of two adult children and grandmother of one, she lives outside of Portland with her golden retriever, Charlie. She is currently enrolled in a formation program to become certified as a spiritual director.

Citations

Journey Through Grief:
Chippewa poem from *The Rag and Bone Shop of the Heart*, edited by Robert Bly, Harper Collins, (1993)
Praying Our Goodbyes, Joyce Rupp, OSM, Ave Maria Press (August 1991)
Gates of Prayer for Weekdays at a House of Mourning, Central Conference of American Rabbis (1992)

What Death Can Teach Us About Life
Native American Wisdom, Kent Nerburn, New World Library (January 1993)
And a Sword Shall Pierce Your Heart: Moving from Despair to Meaning After the Death of a Child , Charlotte Mathes, Chiron Publications (September 2006)

Even Good Girls Get the Blues
Life of the Beloved: Spiritual Living in a Secular World, Henri J. M. Nouwen, The Crossroad Publishing Company (1992)
Small Pieces Loosely Joined: A Unified Theory of the Web, David Weinburger, quoted in Joseph R. Myers, *The Search to Belong: Rethinking Intimacy, Community and Small Groups,* Cambridge, MA: Perseus Publishing (2002)

Put the Key in the Ignition
Go In and In: Poems from the Heart of Yoga, Dana Faulds, Peaceable Kingdom Books (August 2002)

Let it Go, Brian Doyle, U.S. Catholic, Vol. 76, No. 1 (January 2011)

Let Your Life Speak: Listening for the Voice of Vocation, Parker Palmer, Jossey-Bass (1999)

Dancing Through the Storm

Yoga the Iyengar Way, Silva Mehta, Mira Mehta, Shyam Mehta, Knopf, 1st edition (April 1990)

Radical Compassion: Finding Christ in the Heart of the Poor, Gary Smith, Loyola Press, First Edition (October 2002)

Yoga Sutras of Patanjali

God Writes Straight with Crooked Lines

"God Says Yes To Me," Kaylin Haught, published in *The Palm of Your Hand,* edited by Steve Kowit, Tilbury House Publishers (1995). For further permissions, contact: Kaylinhaught@yahoo.com

Finding the Grace in Loneliness

The Holy Longing: The Search for a Christian Spirituality, Ronald Rolheiser, Doubleday (1999)

Everything Belongs: The Gift of Contemplative Prayer, Richard Rohr, The Crossroad Publishing Company; Rev Upd edition (March 2003)